A SOLDIER'S LIFE IN

VIKING

A SOLDIER'S LIFE IN
VIKING TIMES

Fiona Corbridge

M018889

W
FRANKLIN WATTS
LONDON • SYDNEY

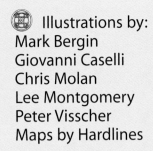 Illustrations by:
Mark Bergin
Giovanni Caselli
Chris Molan
Lee Montgomery
Peter Visscher
Maps by Hardlines

This edition 2007

First published in 2006 by Franklin Watts

Copyright © Franklin Watts 2006

Franklin Watts
338 Euston Road
London NW1 3BH

Franklin Watts Australia
Level 17/207 Kent Street
Sydney NSW 2000

A CIP catalogue record
for this book is available
from the British Library

Dewey classification: 355.00948

ISBN 978 0 7496 7577 6

Printed in China

Franklin Watts is a division of Hachette
Children's Books.

This book is based on
Going to War in Viking Times by
Christopher Gravett © Franklin Watts 2000.
It is produced for Franklin Watts
by Painted Fish Ltd.
Designer: Rita Storey

Series editor: John C. Miles
Art director: Jonathan Hair

CONTENTS

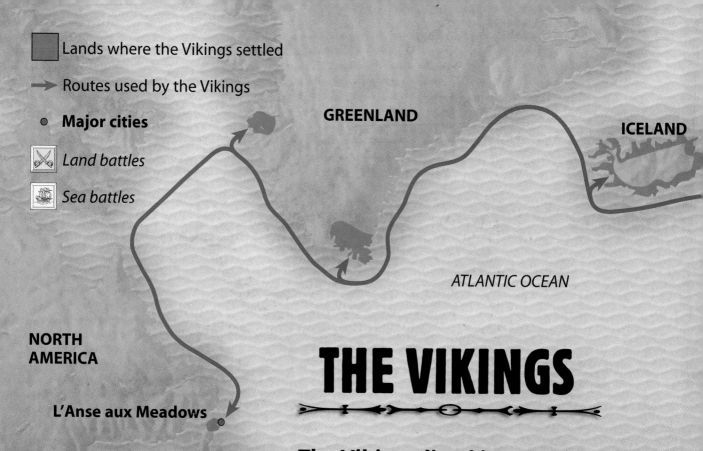

Lands where the Vikings settled

Routes used by the Vikings

• **Major cities**

Land battles

Sea battles

GREENLAND

ICELAND

ATLANTIC OCEAN

NORTH AMERICA

L'Anse aux Meadows

NEWFOUNDLAND

King Alfred of England won battles against the Vikings

THE VIKINGS

The Vikings lived in Norway, Sweden and Denmark. They were a warlike people who often fought each other. They also attacked and stole from people in other countries.

The Vikings were brilliant at building ships. Warriors (soldiers) used these ships to sail on raids to steal gold and other goods. Some Vikings were traders. They sailed to other lands with animals, timber, furs and slaves to sell.

Viking world
In the eighth, ninth and tenth centuries CE, Viking warriors and traders left Scandinavia and went all over the world.

Eighth century – raids on England and Ireland
Viking warriors started to raid England and Ireland. The English did not win a battle against them for 100 years.

Ninth century – raids on Europe
Vikings attacked trading centres in Europe. They sailed up rivers in France and Germany to get there.

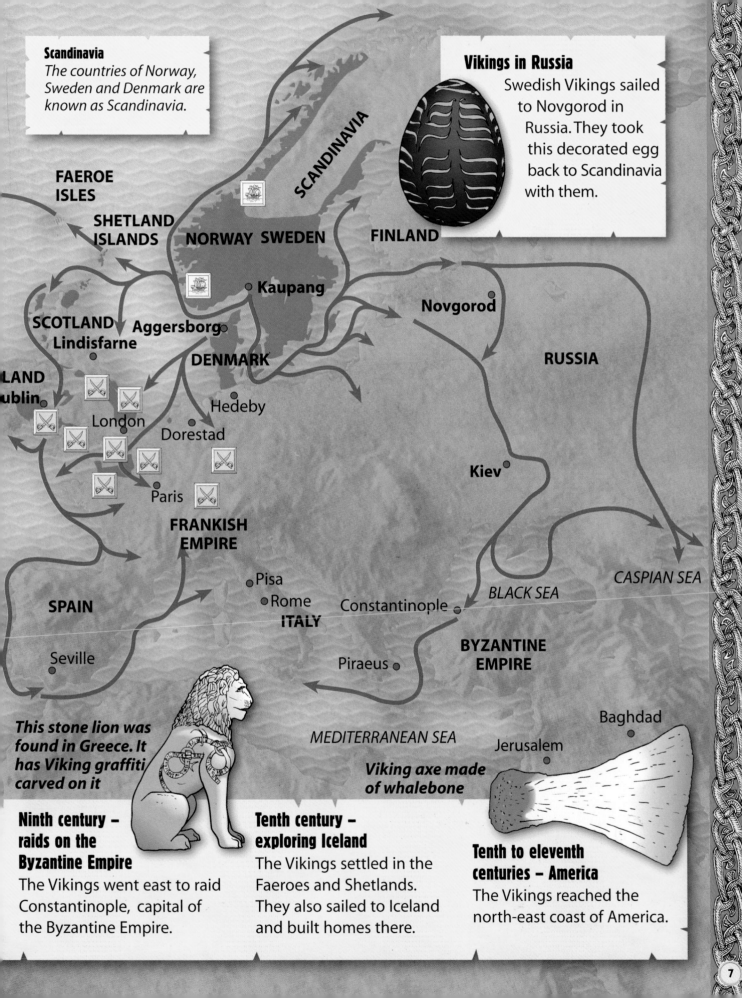

Scandinavia
The countries of Norway, Sweden and Denmark are known as Scandinavia.

Vikings in Russia
Swedish Vikings sailed to Novgorod in Russia. They took this decorated egg back to Scandinavia with them.

FAEROE ISLES

SHETLAND ISLANDS

SCANDINAVIA

NORWAY   SWEDEN   FINLAND

Kaupang

Novgorod

SCOTLAND
Lindisfarne

Aggersborg

DENMARK

RUSSIA

LAND
ublin

London

Hedeby

Dorestad

Kiev

Paris

FRANKISH EMPIRE

Pisa

Rome
ITALY

Constantinople   BLACK SEA   CASPIAN SEA

SPAIN

Seville

BYZANTINE EMPIRE

Piraeus

This stone lion was found in Greece. It has Viking graffiti carved on it

MEDITERRANEAN SEA

Baghdad

Jerusalem

Viking axe made of whalebone

Ninth century – raids on the Byzantine Empire
The Vikings went east to raid Constantinople, capital of the Byzantine Empire.

Tenth century – exploring Iceland
The Vikings settled in the Faeroes and Shetlands. They also sailed to Iceland and built homes there.

Tenth to eleventh centuries – America
The Vikings reached the north-east coast of America.

VIKING WARRIORS

When Viking warriors (soldiers) went into battle or went on raids to other countries, they needed to protect themselves. They wore armour and carried a shield. Rich Vikings had the best armour. Poorer Vikings probably had to fight in their ordinary clothes. They wore a tunic (like a dress), trousers, and a thick cloak to keep warm.

Axe

Helmet

Cloak

Shield

Cloak pin

Chainmail armour

Tunic

Sword

Leather shoes

🔲 CHAINMAIL ARMOUR

Chainmail was made from thousands of iron rings that were linked together. It was made into a coat to protect the body.

🔲 SHIELD

If a warrior was being attacked, he used his shield to try and stop himself getting hurt by his enemy's weapon. Shields were made from wooden boards covered with leather.

FIGHTING BATTLES

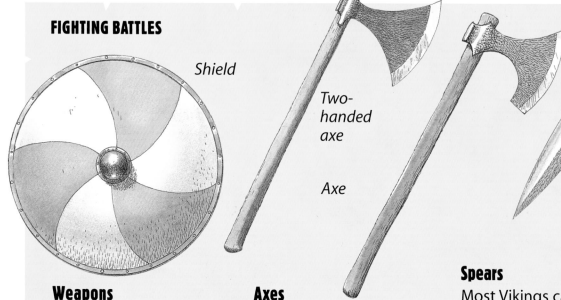

Shield

Two-handed axe

Axe

Spear

Weapons

Vikings had lots of dangerous weapons to fight with – swords, axes, spears and knives. Archers fired arrows from bows two metres tall.

Axes

A two-handed axe was held in both hands. It could easily smash through an enemy's helmet. An ordinary axe was held in one hand.

Spears

Most Vikings carried a spear when they went into battle. A spear was a sharp, pointed blade on a long stick. It could be thrown at enemies, or used to stab them.

An animal's antler carved to look like a Viking warrior

Pommel

Cross-guard

SWORDS

Viking warriors loved their swords and sometimes gave them names such as Leg Biter. Swords had a long blade that was sharp on one edge or both edges.

HELMET

Viking warriors wore a metal helmet to protect the head. It had a long piece at the front to cover the nose. Helmets were either rounded or shaped like a cone.

Double-edged Viking sword

SWORD HILTS

The top part of a sword is called the hilt. The cross-guard helped to protect the warrior's hand. Sometimes the hilt was decorated.

CHIEFTAINS

The Viking people were ruled by lots of chieftains. Each chieftain was in charge of a small area. He had warriors who would fight (and die) for him. The chieftains fought each other to try and get the lands of their neighbours for themselves. By CE 1050, the countries of Scandinavia each had a single king.

THE THING

The important people in a community held a meeting called a Thing to settle arguments and decide other matters. It usually lasted for several days.

A chieftain speaking at a Thing

REWARDS

Viking warriors expected their chieftain to reward them for fighting for him. They wanted to be given land and other goods that were won in battle. If the rewards were not very good, they would go and fight for another chieftain instead. The chieftain's most important warriors were called the *lith*. They lived with him.

FIGHTING DUELS

Vikings often settled arguments by a duel (a fight between two people) called a *holmganga*. The fight would take place on a piece of cloth. If either warrior stepped off the cloth, he lost the duel.

BLOOD MONEY

If someone killed a member of a Viking warrior's family, he could demand money from the murderer to make up for it. This was called blood money.

Fighting a duel

HEROES

Sigurd, a hero of legend

This carving shows a blacksmith making Sigurd a sword to kill a dragon called Fafnir.

Sagas

Long stories about Viking gods and heroes were called sagas. Sagas were eventually written down in manuscripts. Some had paintings like this one.

Viking coin

Wild warriors

The names of some warriors tell us a little about them. Lothbrok Hairy Breeches must have worn rough, hairy trousers. Eric Bloodaxe must have killed lots of enemies with his axe.

A VIKING VILLAGE

People in Viking villages made a living in different ways. Farmers, merchants (traders) and craftspeople were called free people. Peasants (who did not own any land) and *thralls* (slaves) worked for the free people.

In the eighth century, the Vikings started leaving their homes to sail all over the world. Warriors went on raids to fight and steal. Merchants sailed with goods to sell.

Shipbuilders at work

TRADERS

Viking merchants sailed to many foreign ports. They sold walrus tusks for ornaments and boxes, furs for clothing and bedding, wood, amber, falcons and slaves.

A Viking village in Norway

RAIDERS

As well as stealing goods, Viking raiders battled to steal land from other countries. Some Vikings decided to settle (live) in the conquered areas, perhaps because their village was crowded, or because they wanted new land to farm.

SETTLERS

Viking men and women settled in England, Orkney and Shetland Islands, the Isle of Man, Iceland, Greenland and northern France. They built homes and raised families. Sometimes they traded with people living nearby, and sometimes they fought them.

A longship

A raiding party gets ready to sail

Planks to surface the road

Animals and people lived close together

LONGSHIPS

Viking warriors went to war and on raids in ships called longships. These were very strong and could also be used for long journeys to explore other lands. The largest longships were 28 metres long and carried 200–300 warriors. Many longships had a scary carved figurehead on the front in the shape of a dragon's head or mythical animal.

INSIDE A LONGSHIP

A longship had one large sail to catch the wind. If the wind dropped, the warriors used oars to row with. If the weather was bad, they sheltered in a tent on the deck. There were no seats, so when the men had to row, they sat on the chests that held their personal possessions.

Longships were shallow and could sail close to the shore

BUILDING A LONGSHIP

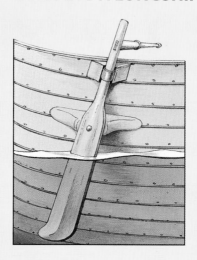

Steering

The ship was steered by a helmsman. He used a steering oar on the right of the ship. Our word "starboard" (steer-board) comes from this. It means the right-hand side of a ship.

Hull of a longship

Hull

The hull (outside shell) of a Viking ship was made from overlapping planks. These were fastened by nails or wooden pegs. Gaps were sealed with rope covered in tar. This sort of hull could bend slightly and rough seas would not damage it. The hull was shallow, so the ship could go near the shore without running aground.

Sail

The sail had a long piece of wood at one corner. The crew moved this to keep the sail in the best position to catch the wind.

TRADING SHIPS

Ships for trading were called *knorrs*. They were slower than longships. The deep shape of a knorr meant that it could carry lots of things. It could hold goods to trade, or it could take people and animals to new lands.

The Vikings also had smaller boats, which they used for short journeys along the coast of their homelands.

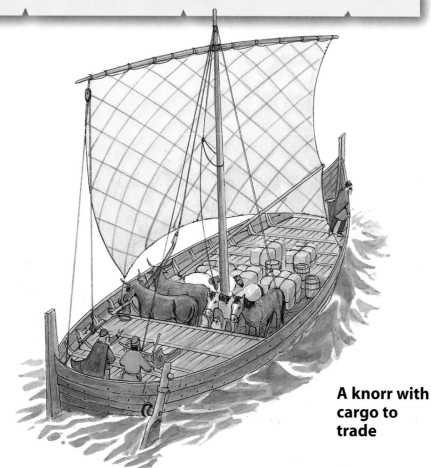

A knorr with cargo to trade

SEA BATTLES AND RAIDS

Viking chieftains often fought each other. They liked to fight sea battles in the sheltered waters of fjords, where it was easy to row the longships. They fixed iron frames to the ships' bows to ram the enemy and put up screens to protect themselves from arrows. Sometimes they tied ships together to make a platform to fight on.

BATTLE OF SVÖLDR

King Olaf Tryggvasson fought a fierce sea battle in CE 1000. His ship, *Long Serpent*, was surrounded by enemies. Olaf's men tried to leap on to the enemies' ships, but many drowned. In the end, Olaf jumped into the sea and drowned himself so that he would not be taken prisoner. This battle is described in a saga.

RIVER RAIDS

The Vikings decided that it was better to raid other countries than to fight each other. They used rivers such as the Rhine in Germany, and the Seine and the Loire in France, to sail inland. They rowed quickly up the rivers, raided towns and left before people could defend themselves.

RAIDS

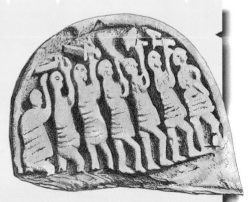

Attack on Lindisfarne
The island of Lindisfarne in north-east England had a famous monastery. People were shocked when Norwegian Vikings attacked it in CE 793.

Looters and raiders
Armed Viking warriors attacked poorly defended towns and villages. They also looted (stole) gold and precious objects from churches and monasteries.

Lindisfarne stone
This stone shows Viking warriors waving axes and swords. No one knows who made it. It may have been used on the grave of someone who died in the monastery attack.

LAND BATTLES

The Vikings fought on foot, not on horseback. Their armies were fairly small. Each chieftain kept his best fighters around him.

Battles began with the exchange of arrows, javelins and insults. Then the two sides closed in for a fierce fight.

BANNERS

Each chieftain had a banner or flag that was carried into battle. Many showed a raven, because it stood for the god Odin. The Vikings believed that Odin decided who won or lost a battle.

Defeated Vikings after a battle

BERSERKIRS

Some warriors were known as *berserkirs*. They usually wore a bearskin. They worked themselves into a frenzy before a battle so that they would not feel pain, and fought madly and fiercely. Kings often had berserkirs as their bodyguards. We get the word "berserk" from them.

THE WAY VIKINGS FOUGHT

Shield fort

To defend themselves, warriors sometimes grouped together with their shields to make a *skjaldborg* (shield fort). This protected them until other warriors arrived.

Island camps

When the Vikings went to war, they found that a small island in the middle of a river made a good base for a camp. This was because it was easy to defend against enemies.

Ladders

Sometimes the enemy hid behind banks, fences and walls. The Vikings used equipment like ladders to scramble up to attack the enemy and get inside these defences.

King Alfred of Wessex

KING ALFRED

The Vikings attacked England many times. But in CE 871, King Alfred of Wessex won his first battle against the Danish Vikings at Ashdown. In 878, his army beat them at Edington. This stopped the Danes taking over the whole of England.

Map showing the Danelaw and neighbouring kingdoms

THE DANELAW

When the Danish Vikings couldn't beat King Alfred, they agreed to stay in one part of England. It was known as the Danelaw. The Danes finally conquered England in CE 1014, led by King Cnut.

MILITARY CAMPS

Soldiers lived in a military camp with their families. From there, they would go off to fight. Camps were protected by high earth walls covered with wood, called ramparts.

In Denmark, archaeologists have found fortified camps at Nonnebakken, Fyrkat, Trelleborg and Aggersborg. They were probably built by King Harald Bluetooth.

INSIDE A MILITARY CAMP

The four camps found by the archaeologists were all near a main road. Each quarter of the camp had four long wooden houses built around a courtyard. This was where the soldiers lived.

Soldiers entered the camp through covered gates. Two roads paved with wood crossed the camp.

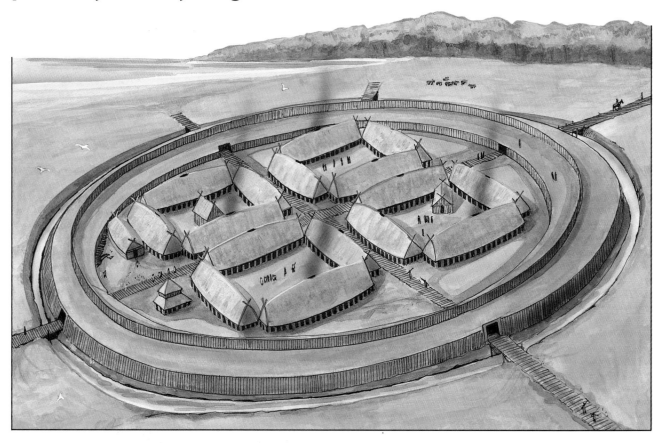

TRELLEBORG CAMP

Trelleborg camp was protected by a large, water-filled ditch and a double wooden palisade (fence). Each of the camp's houses was nearly 30 metres long and had a thatched roof. There was a large living area with a central fireplace. There were also some smaller buildings. Some were used by craftspeople.

VIKING JEWELLERY

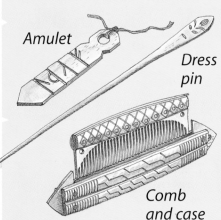

Amulet

Dress pin

Comb and case

Glass beads
Both men and women wore beads. Some beads came from trade with distant lands.

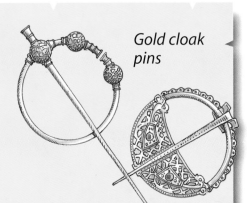

Gold cloak pins

Glass bead necklace

Bone jewellery
Craftspeople carved bone, walrus ivory and antlers to make items such as this amulet, dress pin and comb. The amulet is carved with runes (Viking writing).

Cloak pins
People wore thick cloaks fastened with cloak pins. These were often made from silver or gold and decorated. Men pinned their cloak at the right shoulder so that they could draw their sword easily.

INSIDE A HOUSE
The house had one big room for living and sleeping in. People sat and slept on long wooden benches. In the centre of the room was a hearth where food was cooked over a fire in a large pot called a cauldron. To make fish and meat last for a long time, it could be dried, smoked or salted.

Cauldron over the fire

Hand mill for grinding flour

VIKINGS GO WEST

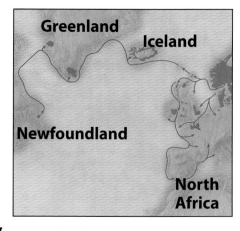

Greenland
Iceland
Newfoundland
North Africa

The Vikings travelled long distances from Scandinavia to raid, trade and settle. They raided England, Scotland, Ireland, France, Germany and the Netherlands. They sailed down to Spain, North Africa, Italy and beyond.

Some Vikings settled in Iceland and Greenland. From here, ships discovered the coast of North America and the island of Newfoundland.

SAILING WEST

In the ninth century, Norwegian Vikings reached Iceland. In the tenth century, Erik the Red sailed to Greenland. His son, Leif, explored the Newfoundland coast.

DANEGELD

Sometimes a king would try to stop the Vikings attacking his country by paying them money. This was called Danegeld. But the Vikings would come back for more.

ATTACKS ON LONDON

London was protected by its old Roman walls (right). In CE 994, Danish Vikings tried to burn the city but failed. In 1016, King Cnut of Denmark tried to capture London. He did not succeed.

ATTACKS ON PARIS

Some towns and cities were protected by ditches or stone walls, but these did not always keep the Vikings out.

In CE 845 a Viking called Ragnar attacked and plundered the city of Paris in France, despite its walls.

In 885–6, a fleet of 700 ships attacked Paris again. Warriors used pickaxes, fire and catapults in the battle.

NORTH AMERICA

Leif Erikson sailed to Newfoundland. He called it Vinland (Wineland) after the huckleberries that grew wild there.

Viking settlers built houses and traded with the Native Americans who lived there. They called the Americans *skraelings* (savages). But before long, fighting broke out between the Vikings and the Americans. After three years, the Vikings decided to sail away.

Native American club with a stone head

VIKINGS GO EAST

As well as travelling west, the Vikings went east. Russia was very close to Sweden, and Swedish Vikings sailed into the country along its rivers.

Other Vikings went south-east as far as Constantinople, the capital of the Byzantine Empire. Here, some of them joined the emperor's bodyguard. They were known as the Varangian Guard.

THE BALTIC SEA
Ships sailing to Russia and Finland used the Baltic Sea to get there.

RUSSIAN RAIDS
Swedish Vikings raided Russian towns that were not well defended. In other places, they traded goods. The cities of Kiev and Novgorod became large trading centres.

VIKING HORSEMEN
When Vikings went to other countries, their clothes began to be influenced by the styles that they saw. This Viking horseman's clothes (especially his trousers and tunic) are like those worn by people in Central Asia.

Swedish Viking horseman in eastern-style clothes

TRADE IN THE EAST

Silver amulet
Traders travelled all over the East. They brought back things like this amulet, which may have come from Baghdad. It perhaps contained spices.

Brazier
A brazier was used to burn charcoal or coal for cooking or heating. Sometimes aromatic spices were burned for their lovely smell.

Bronze Buddha
This statue of Buddha (who founded the religion of Buddhism) was made in India. The Vikings probably used it as an ornament.

RIVER ROUTES
People called Slavs lived along many Russian rivers. Swedish Vikings fought to take control of these communities. The local people called the invaders "Rus". This may be how Russia got its name.

The Vikings used the rivers to sail down to the Black Sea and the Caspian Sea. They went even further to raid and trade. They travelled by foot or by camel to Baghdad, Constantinople and Jerusalem.

Pointed helmet

Stabbing spear

Rus warrior dressed in Central Asian style

Baggy trousers

BATTLE GODS

The Vikings believed in many gods and spirits.

Odin was the god of the dead. He had the power to give victory or defeat in battle. Dead warriors went to live with Odin in his great hall, Valhalla.

Thor was the powerful god of the sky. He protected Asgard, the home of the gods, armed with a mighty hammer called Mjöllnir.

ASKING FOR ODIN'S HELP
Before battle, a warrior would throw a javelin over the enemy. This was to ask Odin to help him win.

TALISMEN

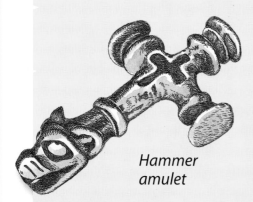

Hammer amulet

Thor
This figure was made in Iceland in about CE 1000. Thor was said to have a red beard. He was sometimes shown riding in a chariot pulled by goats.

Bronze figure of Thor

Thor's hammer
Many Vikings wore a hammer amulet, to represent Thor's hammer. They hoped it would give them protection.

Ragnarök stone
This carving is of a huge battle called Ragnarök, in which the gods were killed. Here Odin is being eaten by his old enemy, the wolf Fenrir.

THE VALKYRIE

The Valkyrie were beautiful female spirits who served Odin. Sometimes they wore armour and rode horses over land and sea. They flew over battlefields to choose dead warriors and take them to live with Odin in Valhalla.

SHIP BURIAL

When a Viking chieftain died, he was sometimes buried in a ship. The Vikings believed that this would take him to the afterlife. He was buried with his possessions. Slaves and horses might also be killed to accompany him. Sometimes the ship was burned so that the chieftain would go to the afterlife quickly.

VIKINGS AND CHRISTIANITY

The Vikings were pagans and believed in gods such as Odin and Thor. When they raided Christian countries, they stole from churches and monasteries.

But then some Viking kings became Christians, and so did their people. Denmark became Christian in about CE 960, when Harald Bluetooth was king. Norway, ruled by King Olaf Haraldsson, followed in about 1024. Sweden stayed pagan until the end of the eleventh century.

BECOMING A CHRISTIAN

Once ordinary people realized that their kings were not punished by the old gods for becoming a Christian, they also decided to be Christians. Many fine wooden churches were built throughout Scandinavia.

BAPTISM

The scene from an altarpiece (right) shows a bishop baptizing King Harald Bluetooth of Norway in a barrel. Baptism is the ceremony where a person is sprinkled with water as a sign that he or she has become a Christian.

CHRISTIAN SYMBOLS

Stave church
Wooden churches, like this one at Borgund in Norway, were built from tree trunks split in two (called staves).

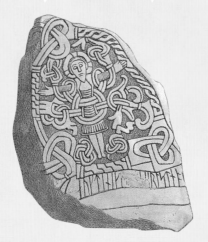

The Jelling stone
After he became a Christian, King Harald Bluetooth put this stone at Jelling in Denmark, in memory of his parents. The stone is the earliest picture of Jesus found in Scandinavia.

Church decoration
Craftspeople carved wooden panels to decorate the stave church at Urnes in Norway. They show ribbon-like beasts biting one another.

 ## THE NORMANS
In CE 911, a Viking called Rollo was given land in France. His followers were called Northmen or Normans. They learnt French and became Christians. In 1066, a descendant of Rollo won the Battle of Hastings and conquered England. He was called William of Normandy.

 ## KNIGHTS ON HORSEBACK
In the twelfth century, the Vikings began to use the same ways of fighting as the people of Europe. Knights were trained to fight from horseback. They carried long shields instead of circular ones.

Norman knight, a descendant of Viking seafarers

GLOSSARY

Eighth century CE = CE 700–799

Ninth century CE = CE 800–899

Tenth century CE = CE 900–999

Eleventh century CE = CE 1000–1099

Twelfth century CE = CE 1100–1199

A date with "BCE" after it means "before the Common Era" or "before the birth of Christ". A date with "CE" before it means "Common Era" or "after the birth of Christ".

Afterlife

The next world, where Vikings believed they went when they died.

Amber

Sap from pine trees that goes solid and is used for jewellery.

Amulet

A piece of jewellery worn to protect against evil.

Archaeologist

A person who studies human history by looking at ancient items that have been discovered, such as bones, the remains of buildings, and possessions.

Berserkir

Warrior who wore a bearskin shirt and fought in a frenzy.

Byzantine Empire

In the third century CE, the Roman Empire was divided into eastern and western parts. The eastern part became the Byzantine Empire. Its capital was Constantinople (Istanbul).

Community

A group of people living together.

Craftspeople

People who are skilled at making certain things.

Danegeld

A kind of ransom paid to invading Danish armies so they would go away.

Danelaw

An area of England where Danish Vikings agreed to stay after making a treaty with King Alfred in 886.

Defence

Protecting a person or place against danger, harm or attack.

Fjord

Long, narrow inlet of sea between high cliffs. It is pronounced "fee-ord".

Fortified

Strengthened. A building is fortified by building walls and fences to protect it.

Franks

A Germanic people who controlled much of western Europe from the sixth century CE. They eventually settled in what we now know as France and Germany.

Knorr

Viking ship with deep sides, for carrying goods and trading.

Legend, legendary

A legend is a story that has been handed down from earlier times. It may or may not be true.

Lith

Group of warriors loyal to their chieftain. They lived with him.

Longship

Slim ship with a shallow hull. It was fast, with a single square sail. It usually had at least thirteen rowers on each side.

Looter

A person who steals money or goods on a raid.

Monastery
A building where a religious community of monks lives away from everybody else.

Myth, mythical
A myth is a story about imaginary (made up) beings or creatures with special powers.

Native American
The original tribal peoples of North America.

Pagan
Someone who has religious beliefs but does not follow one of the main world religions. In Viking times it meant a non-Christian.

Palisade
A strong wooden fence, made of stakes driven into the ground.

Pickaxe
A tool with a pointed metal head and wooden handle.

Rampart
An embankment (ridge of earth or stone) around a fort or military camp, to protect it. It may contain walls or fences.

Raven
A large bird with black feathers and a croaking cry.

Runes
Ancient alphabet used by the peoples of Scandinavia before and during the Viking period. The angular letters were easy to carve on stone and other hard materials.

Sagas
Long stories about the lives and bravery of Viking heroes. To begin with, sagas were told by *skalds* (poets). They were not written down until at least the eleventh century.

Skalds
Viking poets who specialized in reciting sagas and other tales about gods and legendary heroes.

Stave church
An early type of Scandinavian church. To make the walls, logs were split in two and set upright, side by side.

Talisman
A small object carried to protect a person against evil. It was often carved.

Thrall
A slave, often a captive taken by the Vikings in battle or during a raid.

Valhalla
The hall of Odin, the god of the dead. Some dead warriors were taken there to live with Odin. "Valhalla" was sometimes used to mean life after death.

Valkyries
Female servants of Odin who chose which of the warriors killed in battle should be taken to Valhalla to be with Odin. At one time they were feared as demons, but then were thought of as princesses in armour.

Varangian Guard
The Viking warriors who served the Byzantine emperor at Constantinople and formed his bodyguard.

Vinland
"Wineland". The Vikings' name for the area on the coast of North America where they settled. It was probably Newfoundland in Canada. They probably thought the huckleberries that grew there were grapes.

INDEX

➤┤◆├─◯─┤◆├┤

Colourscape folk

16 Designs by Sarah Hatton
using Colourscape Chunky by Kaffe Fassett

The thing that inspired me the most when faced with designing colourscape yarn was the long colour repeat. The yarn embraces the revival of wonderful old techniques in spinning that involve real craftmanship. To see colours fed in to machinery in handfuls of pure colour creating the subtle colourscape blends was very stimulating.

I wanted the palette to be very wearable, from deep mysterious tones of purples, maroons and turquoise to the softness of dusty pastels. Given my idiosyncratic colouring instructions the technicians did a brilliant job of blending our final moods.

Kaffe Fassett

Aiden, Alexis & Finn

Finn & Alexis

Maddy

Abbie

Richie & Polly

Finn, Sonny & Drew

Aiden & Bobbie

Naomi

Poppy

Iris

Jess

Lilly

Richie & Sonny

Sonny & Richie

The Yarn

Kaffe chooses his palette by taking different shades of yarn and knotting them together to inspire the final blend of colours. With Kaffe supervising, the dyed to match wool roving was hand thrown into a trough in his chosen sequences. All wool roving is weighted and measured by hand for accuracy and the process involves careful watching and guiding to make this yarn as Kaffe envisaged. This very unique process is slow, only 300 kilos per machine can be produced in a week. This hands on process uses very special machinery, tooled exclusively for Rowan in Yorkshire, England. After the wool is blended, the yarn is spun, as specified by Kaffe into a soft shetland-like twist for a good handle and generous length. The colours are vibrant in daylight and bring excitement to every stitch.

The Colours

ROWAN
Colourscape

BY KAFFE FASSETT
100% LAMBSWOOL

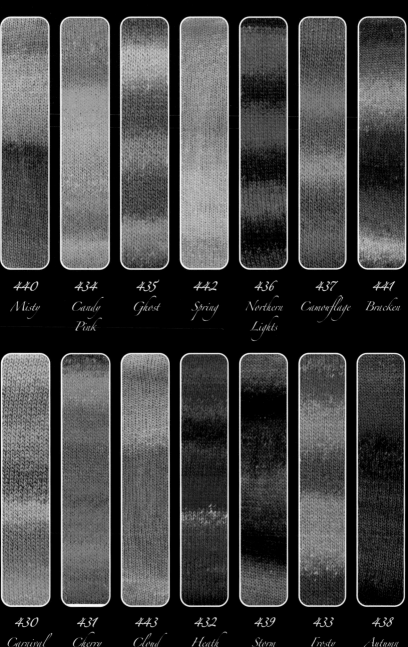

440	*434*	*435*	*442*	*436*	*437*	*441*
Misty	Candy Pink	Ghost	Spring	Northern Lights	Camouflage	Bracken

430	*431*	*443*	*432*	*439*	*433*	*438*
Carnival	Cherry	Cloud	Heath	Storm	Frosty	Autumn

Gallery

Aiden   pattern page 26

Alexis   pattern page 28*

Finn   pattern page 32

Maddy   pattern page 27

Abbie   pattern page 30*

Sonny   pattern page 36

Drew pattern page 40* *Naomi* pattern page 48 *Bobbie* pattern page 38*

Iris pattern page 42 *Jess* pattern page 46* *Lilly* pattern page 52

Polly pattern page 50 *Richie* pattern page 34 *Poppy* pattern page 44

* Buttons for these designs are supplied by Bedecked, please see credit page for contact details

Aiden Hat & Scarf

SIZE

one size

YARN

Rowan Colourscape
| Scarf | 2 | x 100gm |
| Hat | 1 | x 100gm |

(photographed in Storm 439)

NEEDLES

1 pair 7mm (no 2) (US 10½) needles

TENSION

14 sts and 18 rows to 10cm measured over patt using 7mm (US 10½) needles.

SCARF

Cast on 27 sts.

Row 1 (RS): K1, ★ K1, P3, rep from ★ to last 2 sts, K2.

Row 2: K1, P1, ★ K3, P1, rep from ★ to last st, K1.

These 2 rows form rib.

Cont in rib until work meas 165cm, ending with RS facing for next row.

Cast off in rib.

HAT

Cast on 77 sts.

Row 1 (RS): K1, ★ P3, K1, rep from ★ to end.

Row 2: ★ P1, K3, rep from ★ to last st, P1.

These 2 rows form rib.

Cont in rib until work meas 17cm, ending with RS facing for next row.

Shape crown

Next row (RS): ★ K1, P3tog, K1, P3, rep from ★ to last 5 sts, K1, P3tog, K1. 57 sts.

Next row: P1, K1, P1, ★ K3, P1, K1, P1, rep from ★ to end.

Next row: ★ K1, P1, K1, P3, rep from ★ to last 3 sts, K1, P1, K1.

Next row: P1, K1, P1, ★ K3, P1, K1, P1, rep from ★ to end.

Next row:★ K1, P1, K1, P3tog, rep from ★ to last 3 sts, K1, P1, K1. 39 sts.

Next row: ★ P1, K1, rep from ★ to last st, P1.

Next row: K1, ★sl 2tog knitways, K1, p2sso, K1, P1, K1, rep from ★ to last 2 sts, P1, K1. 27 sts.

Next row: P1, K1, P1, ★ K1, P3, rep from ★ to end.

Next row: ★ sl 2 tog knitways, K1, p2sso, P1, rep from ★ to last 3 sts, sl 1, K1, psso, K1. 14 sts.

Next row: ★ P2tog, rep from ★ to end. 7 sts.

Break off yarn and thread through rem sts. Fasten off.

SIZE
one size

YARN
Rowan Colourscape
2 x 100gm
(photographed in Bracken 441)

NEEDLES
1 pair 7mm (no 2) (US 10½) needles

TENSION
14 sts and 18 rows to 10cm measured over patt using 7mm
(US 10½) needles.

Using 7mm (US 10½) needles cast on 23 sts.
Row 1 (RS): K1, ★ P1, K1, rep from ★ to end.
Row 2: ★ P1, K1, rep from ★ to last st, P1.
Row 3: As row 2.
Row 4: As row 1.
These 4 rows form double moss st.
Cont in double moss st as set until work meas 45cm, ending
with **WS** facing for next row.
Next row: Knit, inc 1 st at end of row. 24 sts.
Cont as folls:-

Row 1 (RS): K3, ★ P2, K2, rep from ★ to last st, K1.
Row 2: K1, ★ P2, K2, rep from ★ to last 3 sts, P2, K1.
These 2 rows form rib.
Cont in rib until work meas 109cm, ending with **WS** facing
for next row.
Next row: Knit, dec 1 st at end of last row. 23 sts.
Beg with row 1 of double moss stitch cont until work meas
154 cm, ending with **WS** facing for next row.
Cast off in double moss st.

Alexis

SIZE

	S	M	L	XL	XXL	
To fit bust						
	81–86	91–96	102–107	112–117	122–127	cm
	32–34	36–38	40–42	44–46	48–50	in

YARN

Rowan Colourscape

4	4	5	6	6 x	100gm

(photographed in Storm 439)

NEEDLES

1 pair 7mm (no 2) (US 10½) needles, 1 pair 6mm (no 4) (US 10) needles 6mm (no 4) (US 10) circular needles, Cable needle & Stitch holder

BUTTONS

2 x BN1373 20mm by Bedecked

TENSION

14 sts and 18 rows to 10cm measured over st st using 7mm (US 10½) needles.

SPECIAL ABBREVIATIONS

C4B – slip next 2 sts onto a cable needle and leave at back of work, K2, then K2 from cable needle.

C4F - slip next 2 sts onto a cable needle and leave at front of work, K2, then K2 from cable needle.

BACK

Using 6mm (US 10) needles cast on 66 [74: 82: 94: 100] sts.
Knit 4 rows.

Change to 7mm (US 10½) needles.

Beg with a K row and working in st st throughout, cont until work meas 29 [31: 32: 34: 35]cm, ending with RS facing for next row.

Work 16 [14: 14: 14: 14] rows straight, ending with RS facing for next row. (work should now meas 38 [39: 40: 41: 42]cm)

Next row: K2, M1, K to last 2 sts, M1, K2.
68 [76: 84: 96: 102] sts.

This row sets armhole shaping.

Inc 1 st as set at each end of 2 foll alt rows, then on foll 4th row. 74 [82: 90: 102: 108] sts.

Place markers at each end of last row to denote start of armhole.

Cont straight until armhole meas 25 [26: 27: 28: 29]cm from markers, ending with RS facing for next row.

Shape shoulders and back neck

Next row: Cast off 7 [8: 9: 11: 12] sts, K until there are

21 [24: 26: 30: 31] sts on needle, turn and leave rem sts on a holder.

Work each side of neck separately.

Next row (WS): Cast off 3 sts, P to end.
8 [21: 23: 27: 28] sts.

Next row: Cast off 7 [9: 10: 12: 12] sts, K to end.
11 [12: 13: 15: 16] sts.

Next row: Cast off 3 sts, P to end. 8 [9: 10: 12: 13] sts.
Cast off rem 8 [9: 10: 12: 13] sts.

With RS facing, rejoin yarn to rem sts, cast off centre 18 [18: 20: 20: 22] sts, K to end.

Complete to match first side, reversing all shapings.

LEFT FRONT

Using 6mm (US 10) needles cast on 29 [33: 37: 43: 46] sts.

Row 1 (RS): Knit to last 7 sts, P1, K4, P2.

Row 2: K2, P4, K to end.

Rep these 2 rows once more.

Change to 7mm (US 10½) needles.

Row 1 (RS): Knit to last 7 sts, P1, C4B, P2.

Row 2 and every foll alt row: K2, P4, K1, P to end.

Row 3: Knit to last 7 sts, P1, K4, P2.

Row 5: As row 1.

Row 7: As row 3.

Row 9: As row 3.

Row 10: As row 2.

These 10 rows set st st and cable panel.

Cont until work meas 29 [31: 32: 34: 35]cm, ending with RS facing for next row.

Shape front neck

Next row (RS): K to last 10 sts, K2tog, K1, patt to end. 28 [32: 36: 42: 45] sts.

Next row: Patt to end.

These 2 rows set neck shaping.

Work 14 [12: 12: 12: 12] rows, dec 1 st at neck edge as set on foll 9th [9th: 7th: 7th: 7th] row, ending with RS facing for next row. 27 [31: 35: 41: 44] sts.

(work should now meas 38 [39: 40: 41: 42]cm)

Next row: K2, M1, patt to end. 28 [32: 36: 42: 45] sts.

This row sets armhole shaping shaping.

Inc 1 st as set at side edge on 2 foll alt rows, then on foll 4th row **and at same time** dec 1 st at neck edge on 2nd row. 30 [34: 38: 44: 47] sts.

Place marker at beg of last row to denote start of armhole shaping.

Dec 1 st at neck edge only on 2nd row, then on 3 [5: 5: 5: 5] foll 4th rows, then on 3 [1: 2: 2: 3] foll alt rows. 23 [27: 30: 36: 38] sts.

Cont straight until armhole matches back to start of shoulder shaping, ending with RS facing

Shape shoulder

Next row: Cast off 7 [8: 9: 11: 12] sts, patt to end. 16 [19: 21: 25: 26] sts.

Work 1 row.

Next row: Cast off 7 [9: 10: 12: 12] sts, patt to end. 9 [10: 11: 13: 14] sts.

Work 1 row.

Cast off rem 9 [10: 11: 13: 14] sts and at same time dec 1 st across cable panel.

RIGHT FRONT

Using 6mm (US 10) needles cast on 29 [33: 37: 43: 46] sts.

Row 1 (RS): P2, K4, P1, K to end.

Row 2: K to last 6 sts, P4, K2.

Rep these 2 rows once more.

Change to 7mm (US 10½) needles.

Row 1 (RS): P2, C4F, P1, K to end.

Row 2 and every foll alt row: P to last 7 sts, K1, P4, K2.

Row 3: P2, K4, P1, K to end.

Row 5: As row 1.

Row 7: As row 3.

Row 9: As row 3.

Row 10: As row 2.

These 10 rows set cable panel and st st.

Cont until work meas 29 [31: 32: 34: 35] cm, ending with

RS facing for next row.

Shape front neck

Next row (RS): Patt 7, K1, sl 1, K1, psso, K to end. 28 [32: 38: 44: 47] sts.

Next row: Patt to end.

These 2 rows set neck shaping.

Complete as given for left front, reversing all shapings.

MAKING UP

Press as described on the information page.

Join shoulder seams using back stitch or mattress stitch if preferred.

Buttonband

Using 6mm (US 10) circular needle, pick up and knit 46 [50: 52: 54: 56] sts evenly up right front edge to start of neck shaping, 64 [64: 65: 67: 70] sts up neck shaping, 30 [30: 32: 32: 34] sts from back neck, 64 [64: 65: 67: 70] sts down neck shaping, and 46 [50: 52: 54: 56] sts down left front edge. 250 [258: 266: 274: 286] sts.

Row 1 (WS): P2, ★ K2, P2, rep from ★ to end.

Row 2: ★ K2, P2, rep from ★ to last 2 sts, K2.

These 2 rows set rib.

Work 3 rows more in rib.

Next row (RS) (Buttonhole row): Rib 35 [39: 41: 43: 5], cast off 2 sts, rib 5, cast off 2 sts, rib to end.

Work 6 rows more in rib, casting on 2 sts over gaps left by casting off sts on previous row.

Cast off in rib.

Armhole borders (Both alike)

Using 6mm (US 10) needles pick up and knit 82 [86: 90: 94: 98] sts evenly around armhole edge.

Work 6 rows in rib as set on buttonband.

Cast off in rib.

Join side and underarm seams.

47 [53: 58.5: 67: 71.5]cm
(18½ [21: 23: 26½: 28]in)

71 [73: 75: 77: 79]cm
(28 [28½: 29½: 30½: 31]in)

31

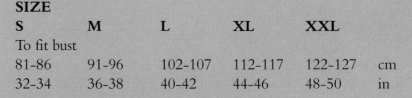

Abbie

SIZE

S	M	L	XL	XXL	
To fit bust					
81-86	91-96	102-107	112-117	122-127	cm
32-34	36-38	40-42	44-46	48-50	in

YARN

Rowan Colourscape

5	5	6	6	7 x	100gm

(photographed in Misty 440)

NEEDLES

1 pair 7mm (no 2) (US 10½) needles, 1 pair 6mm (no 4) (US 10) needles 6mm (no 4) (US 10) circular needle, Stitch holder

BUTTONS

1 x BN1223 by Bedecked

TENSION

14 sts and 18 rows to 10cm measured over st st using 7mm (US 10½) needles.

PATTERN NOTE

If at all possible we suggest trying to begin both the knitted sections with a similarly coloured section of yarn.

BODY (worked in two pieces sideways)
RIGHT SIDE
Using 6mm (US 10) needles cast on 33 [33: 35: 35: 37] sts.
Row 1 (RS): K1, ★ P1, K1, rep from ★ to end.
Row2: ★ P1, K1, rep from ★ to last st, P1.
These 2 rows form rib.
Work 8 rows more in rib.
Change to 7mm (US 10½) needles.
Beg with a K row, working in st st throughout, inc 1 st at each end of 5th row, then 6 [8: 7: 5: 8] foll 8th [6th: 6th: 4th: 4th] rows, then on − [-: 1: 5: 3] foll − [-: 8th: 6th: 6th] rows. 47 [51: 53: 57: 61] sts.
Work 5 [5: 5: 7: 7] rows straight, ending with RS facing for next row.
Inc 1 st at each end of next 4 rows. 55 [59: 61: 65: 69] sts.
Cast on 8 [8: 9: 9: 9] sts at beg of next 8 [8: 10: 10: 8] rows, then cast on 10 [10:-:-:10] sts at beg of 2 [2: -: -: 2] foll rows. 139 [143: 151: 155: 161] sts. ★★
Work 18 [22: 28: 32: 34] rows straight, ending with RS facing for next row.
Cast off 3 sts at beg of next row, then on 2 [2: -: 2: 2] foll alt rows, then 4 sts on − [-: 2: 1: 1] foll alt rows.

130 [134: 140: 142: 148] sts.
Work 1 row, ending with RS facing for next row.
Shape front neck
Next row (RS): Cast off 3 [3: 4: 4: 4] sts, K until there are 58 [59: 61: 61: 64] sts on right needle, turn and leave rem sts on a holder.
Dec 1 st at beg of next row and at same edge on next 13 [13: 14: 14: 14] rows **and at same time** cast off 4 sts at beg of 2nd and 6 foll alt rows. 16 [16: 18: 18: 20] sts.
Work 1 [1: 0: 0: 0] row, ending with RS facing for next row.
Next row (RS): Cast off 4 sts, K to end.
12 [13: 14: 14: 17] sts.
Work 1 row.
Cast off rem 12 [13: 14: 14: 17] sts.
With RS facing, rejoin yarn to rem 69 [72: 75: 77: 80] sts and K to end.
Work 17 rows straight, ending with RS facing for next row.
Leave these sts on a holder.

LEFT SIDE
Work as given for right side to ★★.
Work 19 [23: 29: 33: 35] rows straight, ending with RS facing for next row.
Cast off 3 sts at beg of next row, then on 2 [2: -: 2: 2] foll alt rows, then 4 sts on − [-: 2: 1: 1] foll alt rows.
130 [134: 140: 142: 148] sts.

Work 1 row, ending with RS facing for next row.
Next row: Cast off 3 [3: 4: 4: 4] sts, P until there are
58 [59: 61: 61: 64] sts on right needle and turn, leaving rem
sts on a holder.
Dec 1 st at beg of next row and at same edge on next
13 [13: 14: 14: 14] rows **and at same time** cast off 4 sts at
beg of 2nd and 6 foll alt rows. 16 [16: 18: 18: 20] sts.
Work 1 row, ending with RS facing for next row.
Next row: Cast off 4 sts, P to end. 12 [13: 14: 14: 17] sts.
Cast off rem 12 [13: 14: 14: 17] sts.
With RS facing, rejoin yarn to rem 69 [72: 75: 77: 80] sts and
K to end.
Work 17 rows straight, ending with RS facing for next row.
Leave these sts on a holder.

With RS sides of work held together, cast off both sets of sts
at same time to form back seam.

Neckband

With RS facing, using 6mm (US 10) needles pick up and
knit 14 [14: 14: 15: 15] sts up right side of neck, 32 [32: 32:
34: 34] sts from back neck and 14 [14: 14: 15: 15] sts down
left side of neck. 60 [60: 60: 64: 64] sts.
Row 1 (WS): K1, ★ P2, K2, rep from ★ to last 3 sts, P2, K1.

Row 2: K3, ★ P2, K2, rep from ★ to last st, K1.
These 2 rows set rib.
Cont in rib until neckband meas 8cm, ending with RS
facing for next row.
Cast off in rib.

MAKING UP
Press as described on the information page.
Join side and underarm seams, using back stitch or mattress
stitch if preferred.

Edging
With RS facing, using 6mm (US 10) circular needle pick up
and knit 12 sts from neckband, 96 [98: 100: 102: 104] sts
around front edge, 76 [80: 84: 88: 92] sts along lower back,
96 [98: 100: 102: 104] sts around front edge and 12 sts from
neckband. 292 [300: 308: 316: 324] sts.
Working in rib as set on neckband, work 4 rows.
Next row: Rib 5, cast off 2 sts (to form buttonhole), rib to
end.
Work 5 rows more in rib, casting on 2 sts over cast off sts on
previous row.
Cast off loosely in rib.

Sew on button as shown.

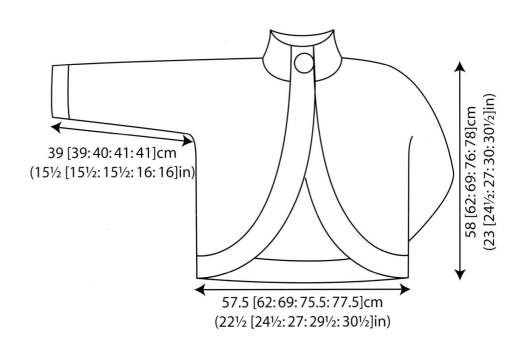

39 [39: 40: 41: 41]cm
(15½ [15½: 15½: 16: 16]in)

58 [62: 69: 76: 78]cm
(23 [24½: 27: 30: 30½]in)

57.5 [62: 69: 75.5: 77.5]cm
(22½ [24½: 27: 29½: 30½]in)

Finn

⬤ ⬤

SIZE

S	M	L	XL	XXL	2XL	
To fit bust						
102	107	112	117	122	127	cm
40	42	44	46	48	50	in

YARN

Rowan Colourscape

6	7	7	7	8	8 x	100gm

(photographed in 438 Autum)

NEEDLES

1 pair 7mm (no 2) (US 10½) needles, 1 pair 6mm (no 4) (US 10) needles
Stitch holder

BUTTONS

5 x BN1369 by Bedecked

TENSION

14 sts and 18 rows to 10cm measured over st st using 7mm (no 2) (US 10½) needles.

BACK
Using 6mm (US 10) needles cast on 77 [81: 85: 91: 97: 101] sts.
Row 1 (RS): ★ K1, P1, rep from ★ to last st, K1.
Row 2: P1, ★ K1, P1, rep from ★ to end.
These 2 rows form 1x1 rib.
Work 10 rows more in rib, dec 1 st at end of last row and ending with RS facing for next row.
76 [80: 84: 90: 96: 100] sts.
Change to 7mm (US 10½) needles.
Beg with a K row cont in st st as follows:
Sizes S, M, L & XL
Inc 1 st at each end of 21st row, then 1 [1: 1: 0] foll 10th row.
80 [84: 88: 92] sts.
All sizes
Cont straight until back meas 40 [41: 40: 41: 40: 41]cm, ending with RS facing for next row.
Shape armholes
Cast off 5 [5: 5: 4: 4: 3] sts at beg of next 2 rows.
70 [74: 78: 84: 88: 94] sts.
Dec 1 st at each end of next 3 [3: 3: 3: 2: 2] rows, then 1 [0: 0: 0: 0: 0] foll alt row. 62 [68: 72: 78: 84: 90] sts.
Cont straight until armholes meas 23 [24: 25: 26: 27: 28]cm, ending with RS facing for next row.
Shape shoulders and back neck
Next row (RS): K until there are 24 [27: 29: 32: 34: 37]sts on needle, turn and leave rem sts on a holder. Work each side of neck separately.
Next row (WS): Cast off 3 sts at beg of next and foll alt

row **and at same time** cast off 9 [10: 11: 13: 14: 15] sts at beg of 2nd row.
Cast off rem 9 [11: 12: 13: 14: 16] sts.
With RS facing, rejoin yarn to rem sts, cast off centre 14 [14: 14: 14: 16: 16] sts and K to end.
Complete to match first side of neck reversing all shapings.

LEFT FRONT
Using 6mm (US 10) needles cast on 38 [40: 42: 46: 48: 50]sts.
Row 1 (RS): ★ K1, P1, rep from ★ to end.
This row forms 1x1 rib.
Work 11 rows more in rib, ending with RS facing for next row, dec 1st at end of last of these rows for size XL only.
[45] sts.
Change to 7mm (US 10½) needles.
Beg with a K row cont in st st throughout as follows.
Sizes S, M, L & XL
Inc 1 st at beg of 21st row, then 1 [1: 1: 0] foll 10th row.
40 [42: 44: 46] sts.
All sizes
Cont straight until front matches back to start of armhole shaping, ending with RS facing for next row.
Shape armholes
Next row (RS): Cast off 5 [5: 5: 4: 4: 3] sts, K to end.
35 [37: 39: 42: 44: 47]sts.
Work 1 row.
Dec 1 st armhole edge of next 3 [3: 3: 3: 2: 2] rows, then 1 [0: 0: 0: 0: 0] foll alt row. 31 [34: 36: 39: 42: 45] sts.
Cont straight until 28 [28: 30: 30: 32: 32] rows less have been

worked than on back to start of shoulder and back neck shaping, ending with RS facing for next row.

Shape front neck

Dec 1 st at end of next row and at same edge of foll 8 rows, then 2 [2: 1: 1: 2: 2] foll alt rows, then 2 [2: 3: 3: 3: 3] foll 4th rows. 18 [21: 23: 26: 28: 31] sts.

Work 7 rows more ending with RS facing for next row.

Shape shoulder

Cast off 9 [10: 11: 13: 14: 15] sts at beg of next row.

Work 1 row.

Cast off rem 9 [11: 12: 13: 14: 16] sts.

RIGHT FRONT

Using 6mm (US 10) needles cast on 38 [40: 42: 46: 48: 50]sts.

Row 1 (RS): ★ P1, K1, rep from ★ to end.

This row forms 1x1 rib.

Work 11 rows more in rib, ending with RS facing for next row, dec 1st at end of last of these rows for size XL only. [45] sts.

Change to 7mm (USA 10½) needles.

Beg with a K row cont in st st throughout.

Work to match left front reversing all shapings

SLEEVES

Using 6mm (US 10) needles cast on 35 [35: 35: 35: 41: 41]sts.

Row 1 (RS): ★ K1, P1, rep from ★ to last st, K1.

Row 2: P1, ★ K1, P1, rep from ★ to end.

These 2 rows form 1x1 rib.

Work 10 rows more in rib, dec 1 st at end of last of these rows and ending with RS facing for next row. 34 [34: 34: 34: 40: 40] sts.

Change to 7mm (US 10½) needles.

Beg with a K row cont in st st throughout, inc 1 st at each end of 7th row, then 0 [0: 4: 3: 0: 0] foll 4th rows, then 11 [11: 9: 10: 11: 13] foll 6th rows. 58 [58: 62: 62: 64: 68] sts.

Cont straight until sleeve meas 53 [55: 57: 59: 61: 62] cm, ending with RS facing for next row.

Shape top

Cast off 5 [5: 5: 4: 4: 3] sts at beg of next 2 rows. 48 [48: 52: 54: 56: 62] sts.

Dec 1 st at each end of next 3 rows, then 3 [3: 3: 3: 4: 9] foll alt rows, then 2 [2: 2: 2: 2: 0] foll 4th rows, then 2 [2: 2: 2: 2: 0] foll alt rows, then 3 foll rows. 22 [22: 26: 28: 28: 32] sts.

Cast off 5 [5: 6: 7: 7: 8] sts at beg of next 2 rows.

Cast off rem 12 [12: 14: 14: 14: 16] sts.

MAKING UP

Press as described on the information page. Join shoulder and side seams, insert sleeves using back st or mattress st if preferred.

Button Band and Collar

With RS facing using 6mm (US 10) needles pick up and knit 75 [79: 77: 79: 77: 81] sts up right front, 36 [36: 38: 38: 40: 40] sts up right front neck, 7 sts down side of back neck, 13 [13: 13: 13: 15: 15] sts from back neck, 7 sts up side of back neck, 36 [36: 38: 38: 40: 40] sts down left front neck and 75 [79: 77: 79: 77: 81] sts down left front.

249 [257: 257: 261: 263: 271] sts.

Beg with Row 2, work 2 rows in rib as given for back.

Next Row (WS): Rib 2 [2: 3: 2: 3: 3], cast off 2 sts, ★ rib 14 [15: 14: 15: 14:15], cast off 2sts, rep from ★ 4 times, rib to end.

Next row: Rib to end casting on 2 sts over cast off sts of button hole row.

Next row: Rib 148 [152: 152: 154: 156: 160], wrap next st (by slipping next st from left needle to right needle, taking yarn to opposite side of work between needles and then slipping st back onto left needle, when working this st on foll rows – work tog the loop and the wrapped st), turn.

Next row: Rib 33, wrap next st and turn.

Next row: Rib 36, wrap next st and turn.

Next row: Rib 39, wrap next st and turn.

Cont as set working 3 extra sts before each wrap st on every row until the following row has been worked;

Next row: Rib 99, wrap next st and turn.

Next row: Patt to end.

Work a further 2 rows across all sts.

Cast off in rib.

Pockets

Using 6mm (US 10) needles cast on 19 sts.

Starting with a K row cont in st st for 12.5cm ending with RS facing for next row.

Starting with row 1 of rib as set for back work 5 rows in rib.

Cast off in rib.

Using photograph as a guide attach pockets.

Sew on buttons.

See information page for finishing instructions.

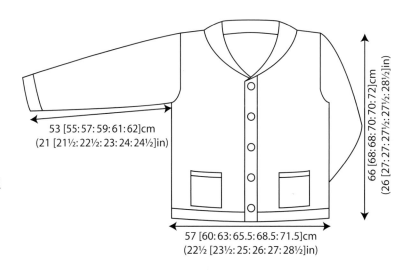

53 [55: 57: 59: 61: 62]cm
(21 [21½: 22½: 23: 24: 24½]in)

66 [68: 68: 70: 70: 72]cm
(26 [27: 27: 27½: 27½: 28½]in)

57 [60: 63: 65.5: 68.5: 71.5]cm
(22½ [23½: 25: 26: 27: 28½]in)

Richie

SIZE

S	M	L	XL	XXL	2XL	
To fit chest						
102	107	112	117	122	127	cm
40	42	44	46	48	50	in

YARN

Rowan Colourscape

5	6	6	7	7	7 x	100gm

(photographed in Storm 439)

NEEDLES

1 pair 7mm (no 2) (US 10½) needles, 1 pair 6mm (no 4) (US 10) needles

TENSION

14 sts and 18 rows to 10cm measured over st st or rib using 7mm (US 10½) needles.

BACK and FRONT (Both alike)

Using 6mm (US 10) needles cast on 77 [81: 85: 89: 93: 97] sts.

Row 1 (RS): P0 [2: 0: 0: 0: 1], K5 [5: 0: 2: 4: 5], ★ P4, K5, rep from ★ to last 0 [2: 4: 6: 8: 1] sts, P0 [2: 4: 4: 4: 1], K0 [0: 0: 2: 4: 0].

Row 2: P0 [0: 0: 2: 4: 0], K0 [2: 4: 4: 4: 1], ★ P5, K4, rep from ★ to last 5 [7: 0: 2: 4: 6] sts, P5 [5: 0: 2: 4: 5], K0 [2: 0: 0: 0: 1].

These 2 rows form rib.

Work 4 rows more in rib, ending with RS facing for next row.

Change to 7mm (US 10½) needles and cont in rib until work meas 41 [42: 41: 42: 41: 42]cm, ending with RS facing for next row.

Shape armholes

Keeping rib correct, cast off 2 sts at beg of next 2 rows.

73 [77: 81: 85: 89: 93] sts.

Dec 1 st at each end of next row then 2 foll alt rows.

67 [71: 75: 79: 83: 87] sts.

Cont straight until armhole meas 24 [25: 26: 27: 29] cm, ending with RS facing for next row.

Shape shoulders and back neck

Cast off 9 [10: 11: 12: 12: 13] sts at beg of next 2 rows.

49 [51: 53: 55: 59: 61] sts.

Cast off 10 [11: 11: 12: 13: 14] sts at beg of next 2 rows.

29 [29: 31: 31: 33: 33] sts.

Work 2 rows, ending with RS facing for next row.

Dec 1 st at each end of next and foll 4th row.

25 [25: 27: 27: 29: 29] sts.

Cont straight until work meas 6 cm from cast off sts at shoulders, ending with RS facing for next row.

Cast off in rib.

SLEEVES

Using 6mm (US 10) needles cast on 33 [33: 35: 35: 37: 37] sts.

Row 1 (RS): K1 [1: 2: 2: 3: 3], ★ P4, K5, rep from ★ to last 5 [5: 6: 6: 7: 7] sts, P4, K1 [1: 2: 2: 3: 3].

Row 2: P1 [1: 2: 2: 3: 3], K4, ★ P5, K4, rep from ★ to last 1 [1: 2: 2: 3: 3] sts, P1 [1: 2: 2: 3: 3].

These 2 rows form rib.

Work 4 rows more in rib, ending with RS facing for next row.

Change to 7mm (US 10½) needles and cont in rib throughout, inc 1 st at each end of 7th row, then every foll 6th [6th: 6th: 8th: 6th:6th] row to 43 [41: 39: 59: 53: 51] sts, then every foll 8th [8th: 8th: - : 8th :8th] row to 57 [57: 59: -: 65: 65] sts.

Cont straight until sleeve meas 53 [55: 57: 59: 61: 63]cm, ending with RS facing for next row.

Shape sleeve top

Keeping rib correct, cast off 2 sts at beg of next 2 rows.

53 [53: 55: 55: 61: 61] sts.

Dec 1 st at each end of next row, then 2 foll alt rows.

47 [47: 49: 49: 55: 55] sts.

Work 1 row.

Cast off 6 sts at beg of next 6 rows. 11 [11: 13: 13: 19: 19] sts.

Cast off rem 11 [11: 13: 13: 19: 19] sts in rib.

MAKING UP

Press as described on the information page.

Join both shoulder and neckband seams using back stitch or mattress stitch if preferred.

See information page for finishing instructions, setting in sleeves using the setting in method.

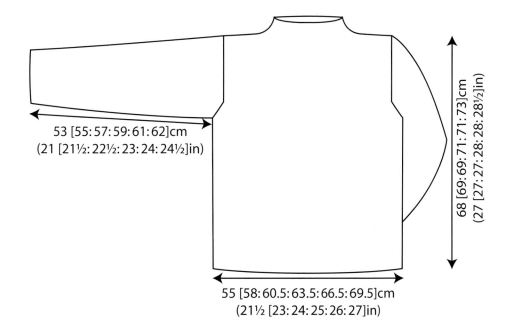

53 [55: 57: 59: 61: 62]cm
(21 [21½: 22½: 23: 24: 24½]in)

68 [69: 69: 71: 71: 73]cm
(27 [27: 27: 28: 28: 28½]in)

55 [58: 60.5: 63.5: 66.5: 69.5]cm
(21½ [23: 24: 25: 26: 27]in)

Sonny

SIZE

S	M	L	XL	XXL	2XL	
To fit chest						
102	107	112	117	122	127	cm
40	42	44	46	48	50	in

YARN

Rowan Colourscape

3	3	4	4	4	4 x	100gm

(photographed in Camouflage 437)

NEEDLES

1 pair 7mm (no 2) (US 10½) needles, 1 pair 6mm (no 4) (US 10) needles
1 6mm (no 4) (US 10) circular needle, Stitch holder

TENSION

14 sts and 18 rows to 10cm measured over st st using 7mm (US 10½) needles.

BACK
Using 6mm (US 10) needles cast on 71 [75: 79: 83: 87: 91] sts.
Row 1 (RS): ★ K1, P1, rep from ★ to last st, K1.
Row 2: P1, ★ K1, P1, rep from ★ to end.
These 2 rows form 1x1 rib.
Work 10 rows more in rib, ending with RS facing for next row.
Change to 7mm (US 10½) needles.
Beg with a K row and working in st st throughout, work 4 rows, ending with RS facing for next row.
Next row (RS): K2, M1, K to last 2 sts, M1, K2.
73 [77: 81: 85: 89: 93] sts.
This row sets side seam shaping.
Inc 1 st as set at each end of 2 foll 12th rows.
77 [81: 85: 89: 93: 97] sts.
Cont straight until work meas 36 [37: 36: 37: 36: 37]cm, ending with RS facing for next row. *65 rows.*
Shape armholes
Cast off 7 sts at beg of next 2 rows. 63 [67: 71: 75: 79: 83] sts.
Dec 1 st at each end of next 5 [3: 1: 1: 1: 1] rows, then on 2 [3: 4: 4: 3: 1] foll alt rows, then on − [−: −: −: 1: 2] foll 4th rows. 49 [55: 61: 65: 69: 75] sts.
Cont straight until armhole meas 24 [25: 26: 27: 28: 29]cm, ending with RS facing for next row. *45 rows*
Shape shoulders and back neck

Next row (RS): Cast off 6 [7: 8: 9: 10: 11] sts, K until there are 9 [11: 12: 13: 13: 15] sts on right needle, turn and leave rem sts on a holder.
Work each side of neck separately.
Next row (WS): Cast off 3 sts, P to end.
6 [8: 9: 10: 10: 12] sts.
Cast off rem 6 [8: 9: 10: 10: 12] sts.
With RS facing, rejoin yarn to rem sts, leave centre 19 [19: 21: 21: 23: 23] sts on a holder, K to end.
Complete to match first side reversing all shapings.

FRONT
Work as given for Back to start of armhole shaping, ending with RS facing for next row.
Shape armholes and front neck
Next row: Cast off 7 sts, K until there are 31 [33: 35: 37: 39: 41] sts on needle, turn and leave rem sts on a holder.
Work 1 row. ✓
Dec 1 st at armhole edge on next 5 [3: 1: 1: 1: 1] rows, then on 2 [3: 4: 5: 3: 1] foll alt rows, then on − [−: −: −: 1: 2] foll 4th rows **and at same time** dec 1 st at neck edge on next and every foll alt row. 19 [22: 25: 25: 28: 31] sts.
Dec 1 st at neck edge only on 2nd and foll alt [alt: alt: −: −: −] rows, then on every foll 4th row to 12 [15: 17: 19: 20: 23] sts.
Cont straight until armhole matches back to start of shoulder shaping, ending with RS facing for next row.

Shape shoulder

Next row (RS): Cast off 6 [7: 8: 9: 10: 11] sts, K to end.
Work 1 row.
Cast off rem 6 [8: 9: 10: 10: 12] sts.
With RS facing, leave centre st on a safety pin, rejoin yarn to rem sts and knit to end.
Complete to match first side reversing all shapings.

MAKING UP

PRESS as described on the information page.
Join right shoulder seam.

Neckband

With RS facing, using 6mm (US 10) circular needle pick up and knit 38 [40: 42: 44: 46: 48] sts down left side of neck, 1 st from safety pin at front neck and mark this st with a coloured thread, 38 [40: 42: 44: 46: 48] sts up right side of neck, 2 sts down side of back neck, 19 [19: 21: 21: 23: 23] sts from holder at back neck and 2 sts up side of back neck.
100 [104: 110: 114: 120: 124] sts.
Round 1 (RS): *K1, P1, rep from * to within 2 sts of marked st, K1, slip next 2 sts tog as though to K2tog (marked

st is 2nd of these 2 sts), K1, pass 2 slipped sts over, **K1, P1, rep from ** to end.
This round sets position of rib.
Keeping rib correct, cont as folls:
Round 2: Rib to within 1 st of marked st, slip next 2 sts tog as though to K2tog (marked st is 2nd of these 2 sts), K1, pass 2 slipped sts over, rib to end.
Rep last round 3 times more. 90 [94: 100: 104: 110: 114] sts.
Cast off in rib, still decreasing either side of marked st as before.

Armhole borders (both alike)

With RS facing, using 6mm (US 10) needles, pick up and knit 77 [81: 83: 87: 89: 93] sts evenly all round armhole edge.
Beg with row 2, work in rib as given for back for 5 rows, ending with RS facing for next row.
Cast off in rib.
See information page for finishing instructions.

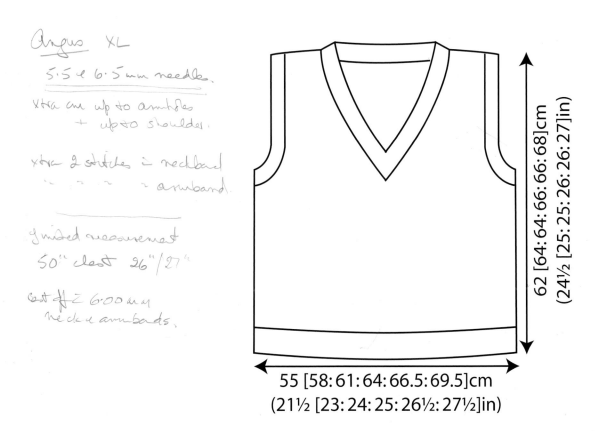

Angus XL
5.5 & 6.5 mm needles.
Xtra cm up to armholes
+ up to shoulder.

xtra 2 stitches in neckband
" " " " " armband.

finished measurement
50" chest 26"/27"

Cast off ≥ 6·00 mm
neck & armbands.

62 [64: 64: 66: 66: 68]cm
(24½ [25: 25: 26: 26: 27]in)

55 [58: 61: 64: 66.5: 69.5]cm
(21½ [23: 24: 25: 26½: 27½]in)

Bobbie

SIZE

S	M	L	XL	XXL	
To fit bust					
81-86	91-96	102-107	112-117	122-127	cm
32-34	36-38	40-42	44-46	48-50	in

YARN

Rowan Colourscape

4	4	5	5	6 x	100gm

(photographed in Autumn 438)

NEEDLES

1 pair 7mm (no 2) (US 10½) needles, 1 pair 6mm (no 4) (US 10) needles
Stitch holder

BUTTONS

1 x BN1369 by Bedecked

TENSION

14 sts and 18 rows to 10cm measured over patt using 7mm (US 10½) needles.

BACK

Using 7mm (US 10½) needles cast on 65 [73: 81: 89: 99] sts.
Row 1 (RS): K1 ★ P1, K1, rep from ★ to end.
Row 2: ★ P1, K1, rep from ★ to last st, P1.
Row 3: As row 2.
Row 4: As row 1.
These 4 rows form patt.
Work 4 [6: 8: 10: 12] rows more, ending with RS facing.
Dec 1 st at each end of next and 2 foll 6th rows.
59 [67: 75: 83: 93] sts.
Work 9 rows straight, ending with RS facing for next row.
Inc 1 st at each end of next and 2 foll 8th rows, working inc sts in patt. 65 [73: 81: 89: 99] sts.
Cont in patt until back meas 34 [35: 36: 37: 38] cm, ending with RS facing for next row.
Shape armholes
Keeping patt correct, cast off 4 [5: 6: 7: 8] sts at beg of next 2 rows. 57 [63: 69: 75: 83] sts.
Dec 1 st at each end of next 3 [5: 7: 5: 9] rows, then on 1 [1: 0: 2: 0] foll alt rows. 49 [51: 55: 61: 65] sts.
Cont straight until armholes meas 21 [22: 23: 24: 25]cm, ending with RS facing for next row.
Shape shoulders
Cast off 5 [6: 6: 8: 8] sts at beg of next 2 rows.
39 [39: 43: 45: 49] sts.
Cast off 6 [6: 7: 8: 9] sts at beg of next 2 rows.

27 [27: 29: 29: 31] sts
Cast off rem 27 [27: 29: 29: 31] sts in patt.

LEFT FRONT

Using 7mm (US 10½) needles cast on 37 [41: 45: 49: 53] sts.
Working in patt as given for back throughout cont as folls:
Work 8 [10: 12: 14: 16] rows, ending with RS facing for next row.
Dec 1 st at beg of next and 2 foll 6th rows.
34 [38: 42: 46: 50] sts.
Work 9 rows straight, ending with RS facing for next row.
Inc 1 st at beg of next and 2 foll 8th rows, working inc sts in patt. 37 [41: 45: 49: 53] sts.
Cont straight until left front matches back to start of armhole shaping, ending with RS facing for next row.
Shape armhole
Next row (RS): Keeping patt correct, cast off 4 [5: 6: 7: 8] sts, patt to end. 33 [36: 39: 42: 45] sts.
Work 1 row.
Dec 1 st at armhole edge of next 3 [5: 7: 5: 9] rows, then on 1 [1: 0: 2: 0] foll alt rows. 29 [30: 32: 35: 36] sts.
Cont straight until armhole meas 21 [22: 23: 24: 25]cm, ending with RS facing for next row.
Shape shoulder
Next row (RS): Cast off 5 [6: 6: 8: 8] sts, patt to end.
24 [24: 26: 27: 28] sts.

Work 1 row.
Next row: Cast off 6 [6: 7: 8: 9] sts, patt to end.
18 [18:19:19:19] sts.
Cast off rem 18 [18:19:19:19] sts in patt.

RIGHT FRONT
Work as given for left front, reversing all shapings.

SLEEVES
Using 7mm (US 10½) needles cast on 49 [55: 57: 61: 67] sts.
Work 4 rows in patt as given for back, ending with RS facing for next row.
Shape sleeve top
Keeping patt correct, cast off 4 [5: 6: 7: 8] sts at beg of next 2 rows. 41 [45: 45: 47: 51] sts.
Dec 1 st at each end of next 5 [5: 5: 5: 7] rows, then on every foll alt row to 23 [25: 21: 17: 21] sts, then on 5 [5: 3: 1: 3] foll

rows. 13 [15: 15: 15: 15] sts.
Cast off 3 sts at beg of next 2 rows. 7 [9: 9: 9: 9] sts.
Cast off rem 7 [9: 9: 9: 9] sts in patt.

MAKING UP
Press as described on the information page.
Back neck edging
With RS facing, using 6mm (US 10) needles, pick up and knit 27 [27: 29: 29: 31] sts across back neck.
Cast off knitways (on **WS**).
Button Loop
Using 6mm (US 10) needles cast on 11 sts.
Cast off.

Join shoulder seams. Join side seams and sew in sleeves using the set in method. Sew button loop and button in position.

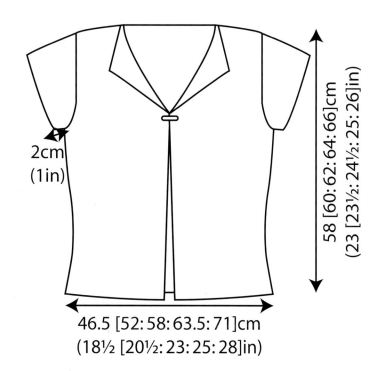

2cm
(1in)

58 [60: 62: 64: 66]cm
(23 [23½: 24½: 25: 26]in)

46.5 [52: 58: 63.5: 71]cm
(18½ [20½: 23: 25: 28]in)

MISTY — MED. SIZE.
C.on ē 8M 2needle — 1st row into back of stitches.

68 rows to armhole

armhole — 45 rows.

Drew

SIZE

	S	M	L	XL	XXL	
To fit bust						
	81–86	91–96	102–107	112–117	122–127	cm
	32–34	36–38	40–42	44–46	48–50	in

YARN

Rowan Colourscape

4	4	4	5	6 x	100gm

(photographed in Misty 440)

NEEDLES

1 pair 7mm (no 2) (US 10½) needles, 1 pair 6mm (no 4) (US 10) needles
Stitch holder

BUTTONS

2 x BN1369 by Bedecked

TENSION

14 sts and 18 rows to 10cm measured over st st using 7mm (no 2)
(US 10½) needles.

BACK

Using 6mm (US 10) needles cast on 64 [72: 80: 88: 98] sts.
Knit 2 rows.
Change to 7mm (US 10½) needles.
Beg with a K row, cont in st st, work 8 [8: 10: 14: 16] rows,
ending with RS facing for next row.
Dec 1 st at each end of next and foll 6th row.
60 [68: 76 :84: 94] sts.
Work 9 rows straight, ending with RS facing for next row.
Inc 1 st at each end of next and foll 8th row.
64 [72: 80: 88: 98] sts.
Cont straight until back meas 30 [31: 32: 33: 34]cm, ending
with RS facing for next row.

59 rows

Place a marker at each end of last row.
Work 6 rows more, ending with RS facing for next row.
Shape armholes
Cast off 4 [5: 6: 7: 8] sts at beg of next 2 rows.
56 [62: 68: 74: 82] sts.
Dec 1 st at each end of next 3 [5: 5: 7: 7] rows, then 1 [1: 2:
1: 2] foll alt rows.
48 [50: 54: 58: 64] sts.
Cont straight until armholes meas 21 [22: 23: 24: 25] cm,
ending with RS facing for next row.
Shape shoulders
Cast off 3 sts at beg of next 2 rows. 42 [44: 48: 52: 58] sts.
Cast off rem 42 [44: 48: 52: 58] sts.

LEFT FRONT

Using 6mm (US 10) needles cast on 37 [41: 45: 49: 54] sts.
Knit 2 rows.
Change to 7mm (US 10½) needles.
Next row (RS): Knit to last 11 sts, leave rem 11 sts on a
holder, turn and cont on these 26 [30: 34: 38: 43] sts only.
Cont in st st, work 7 [7: 9: 13: 15] rows, ending with RS
facing for next row.
Dec 1 st at beg of next and foll 6th row. 24 [28: 32: 36: 41] sts.
Work 9 rows straight, ending with RS facing for next row.
Inc 1 st at beg of next and foll 8th row. 26 [30: 34: 38: 43] sts.
Cont straight until left front matches back to markers, ending
with RS facing for next row.
Shape neck
Dec 1 st at neck edge in next 1 [1: 1: 1: 6] rows, then on 2 [2:
2: 2: 0] foll alt rows, ending with RS facing for next row.
23 [27: 31: 35: 37] sts.
Work 1 [1: 1: 1: 0] rows more, ending with RS facing for
next row.
Shape armhole
Next row (RS): Cast off 4 [5: 6: 7: 8] sts, K to last 2 sts,
K2tog. 18 [21: 24: 27: 28] sts.
Work 1 row.
Dec 1 st at armhole edge on next 3 [5: 5: 7: 7] rows, then
1 [1: 2: 1: 2] foll alt rows **and at same time** dec 1 st at neck
edge on next row, then 2 [3: 4: 4: 5] foll alt rows.

11 [11: 12: 14: 13] sts.

Dec 1 st at neck edge only on 2nd row, then every foll alt row to 6 [6: 5: 3: 3] sts, then every foll 4th [4th: 4th: –: –] row to 3 [3: 3: –: –] sts.

Cont straight until left front matches back to start of shoulder shaping, ending with RS facing for next row.

Cast off rem 3 sts.

RIGHT FRONT

Using 6mm (US 10) needles cast on 37 [41: 45: 49: 54] sts.

Knit 2 rows.

Change to 7mm (US 10½) needles.

Next row (RS): K 11 sts, leave these 11 sts on a holder, K to end and cont on these 26 [30: 34: 38: 43] sts only.

Complete to match left front, reversing all shapings.

MAKING UP

Press as described on the information page.

Join shoulder seams using back stitch or mattress stitch if preferred.

Left front edging

With RS facing using 6mm (US 10) needles, rejoin yarn to 11 sts left on a stitch holder and cont in g st until left front edging is long enough when slightly stretched to to fit to centre back neck, ending with RS facing for next row.

Cast off. Slip stitch in position.

Right front edging

With **WS** facing using 6mm (US 10) needles rejoin yarn to 11 sts left on a stitch holder and cont in g st until 4 rows below start of neck decreases, ending with RS facing for next row.

Next row (RS)(Buttonhole row): K2, K2tog, yrn, K3, K2tog, yrn, K2.

Cont in g st until left front edging is long enough when slightly stretched to to fit to centre back neck, ending with RS facing for next row.

Cast off. Slip stitch in position.

Armhole borders (Both alike)

With RS facing, using 6mm (US 10) needles, pick up and knit 74 [78: 84: 89: 94] sts evenly all round armhole edge.

Knit 2 rows.

Cast off knitways (on **WS**).

Join side seams.

Sew on buttons.

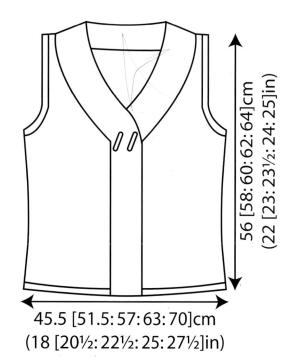

45.5 [51.5: 57: 63: 70]cm
(18 [20½: 22½: 25: 27½]in)

56 [58: 60: 62: 64]cm
(22 [23: 23½: 24: 25]in)

Iris

SIZE

S	M	L	XL	XXL	
To fit bust					
81-86	91-96	102-107	112-117	122-127	cm
32-34	36-38	40-42	44-46	48-50	in

YARN

Rowan Colourscape

4	5	5	5	6 x	100gm

(photographed in Heath 432)

NEEDLES

1 pair 7mm (no 2) (US 10½) needles, 1 pair 6mm (no 4) (US 10) needles
Stitch holder

TENSION

14 sts and 18 rows to 10cm measured over st st using 7mm (no 2) (US 10½) needles.

SPECIAL ABBREVIATIONS

Tw2 – K into front of 2nd st on left needle, then K first st and slip both sts off left needle together.

BACK

Using 6mm (US 10) needles cast on 67 [73: 83: 91: 99] sts.
Row 1 (RS): K1, ★ P1, K1, rep from ★ to end.
Row 2: ★ P1, K1, rep from ★ to last st, P1.
These 2 rows form 1 x 1 rib.
Work 2 rows more in rib, inc 1 st at end of last row.
68 [74: 84: 92: 100] sts.
Change to 7mm (US 10½) needles.
Beg with a K row and working in st st throughout, cont until work meas 32 [33: 34: 35: 36] cm, ending with RS facing for next row. ★★
Work 2 [2: 2: 2: 2] rows more.
Shape armholes
Cast off 4 [5: 6: 7: 8] sts at beg of next 2 rows.
60 [64: 72: 78: 84] sts.
Dec 1 st at each end of next 3 [5: 7: 7: 9] rows, then on 2 [1: 1: 2: 1] foll alt rows. 50 [52: 56: 60: 64] sts.
Cont straight until armhole meas 21 [22: 23: 24: 25]cm, ending with RS facing for next row.
Shape shoulders and back neck
Next row: Cast off 5 [6: 6: 7: 8] sts, K until there are 9 [9: 10: 11: 11] sts on needle, turn and leave rem sts on a holder.
Work each side of neck separately.
Next row (WS): Cast off 3 sts, P to end. 6 [6: 7: 8: 8] sts.
Cast off rem 6 [6: 7: 8: 8] sts.
With RS facing, leave centre 22 [22: 24: 24: 26] sts on a holder, rejoin yarn to rem sts and knit to end.
Complete to match first side, reversing all shapings.

FRONT

Work as given for back to ★★.
Next row: K17 [20: 25: 29: 33], (P2, Tw2) 8 times, P2, K to end.
Next row: P17 [20: 25: 29: 33], K2, (P2, K2) 8 times, P to end.
These 2 rows set patt panel, cont in patt as set throughout as follows:
Shape armholes
Keeping patt correct, cast off 4 [5: 6: 7: 8] sts at beg of next 2 rows. 60 [64: 72: 78: 84] sts.
Dec 1 st at each end of next 3 [5: 7: 7: 9] rows, then on 2 [1: 1: 2: 1] foll alt rows. 50 [52: 56: 60: 64] sts.
Cont straight until 16 [16: 18: 18: 20] rows less have been worked than on back to start of shoulder shaping, ending with RS facing for next row.
Shape front neck
Next row: Patt 18 [19: 21: 23: 25], turn and leave rem sts on

a holder.

Work each side of neck separately.

Work 1 row.

Dec 1 st at neck edge in next 5 rows, then 1 [1: 2: 2: 3] foll alt rows, then on foll 4th row. 11 [12: 13: 15: 16] sts.

Work 3 rows straight, ending with RS facing for next row.

Shape shoulder

Next row: Cast off 5 [6: 6: 7: 8] sts, patt to end.

Work 1 row.

Cast off rem 6 [6: 7: 8: 8] sts.

With RS facing, leave centre 14 sts on a holder, rejoin yarn to rem sts and knit to end.

Complete to match first side reversing all shapings.

SLEEVES

Using 6mm (US 10) needles cast on 47 [47: 49: 49: 51] sts.

Work 4 rows in rib as given for back.

Change to 7mm (US 10½) needles.

Beg with a K row and working in st st throughout, cont until work meas 24 [25: 26: 26: 26] cm, ending with RS facing for next row.

Shape sleeve top

Cast off 4 [5: 6: 7: 8] sts at beg of next 2 rows.

39 [37: 37: 35: 35] sts.

Dec 1 st at each end of next 5 [5: 3: 1: 3] rows, then on

6 [7: 10: 11: 11] foll alt rows, then foll 5 [3: 1: 1: 1] row, 5 ending with RS facing for next row. 7 [7: 9: 9: 5] sts.

Cast off rem 7 [7: 9: 9: 5] sts.

MAKING UP

Press as described on the information page.

Join right shoulder seam using back stitch or mattress stitch if preferred.

Polo neck

Using 6mm (US 10) needles, pick up and knit 14 [14: 15: 15: 18] sts evenly down left side of neck, 14 sts from holder at front neck, 14 [14: 15: 15: 18] sts evenly up right side of neck, 3 sts down side of back neck, 22 [22: 24: 24: 26] sts from holder at back neck and 3 sts up side of back neck. 70 [70: 74: 74: 82] sts.

Row 1 (RS of collar, WS of work): ★ P2, Tw2, rep from ★ to last 2 sts, P2.

Row 2: K2, ★ P2, K2, rep from ★ to end.

These 2 rows form patt.

Cont in patt until collar meas 17 cm, ending with **WS** facing for next row.

Cast off in patt.

See information page for finishing instructions.

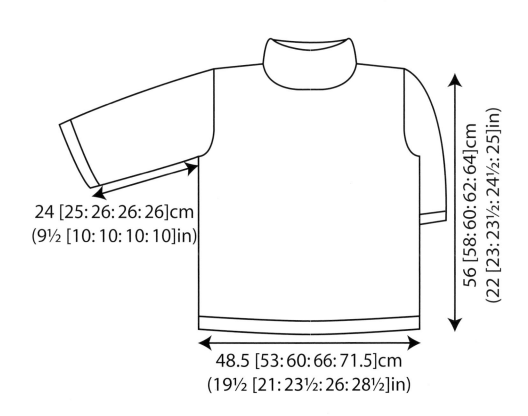

24 [25: 26: 26: 26]cm
(9½ [10: 10: 10: 10]in)

56 [58: 60: 62: 64]cm
(22 [23: 23½: 24½: 25]in)

48.5 [53: 60: 66: 71.5]cm
(19½ [21: 23½: 26: 28½]in)

Poppy

SIZE

S	M	L	XL	XXL	
To fit bust					
81–86	91–96	102–107	112–117	122–127	cm
32–34	36–38	40–42	44–46	48–50	in

YARN

Rowan Colourscape

5	5	6	6	7 x	100gm

(photographed in 443 Cloud)

NEEDLES

1 pair 7mm (no 2) (US 10½) needles, 1 pair 6mm (no 4) (US 10) needles
Stitch holder

TENSION

15 sts and 17 rows to 10cm measured over patt using 7mm (US 10½) needles.

BACK

Using 6mm (US 10) needles cast on 79 [85: 93: 103: 111] sts.
Knit 2 rows.
Change to 7mm (US 10½) needles and cont as folls:
Row 1 (RS): K3 [0: 4: 3: 1], K2togtbl, ★ K4, (K1, yon, K1)
into next st, K4, sl 1, K2tog, psso, rep from ★ to last
14 [11: 15: 14: 12] sts, K4, (K1, yon, K1) into next st, K4,
K2tog, K3 [0: 4: 3: 1].
Row 2: Purl.
These 2 rows form patt.
Cont in patt until back meas 36 [37: 38: 39: 40] cm, ending
with RS facing for next row.
Place a marker at each end of last row to denote start of
armhole.
Cont straight until armholes meas 22 [23: 24: 25: 26] cm,
ending with RS facing for next row.
Shape shoulders
Next row (RS): Keeping patt correct, cast off 10 [12: 13:
16: 17] sts, patt until there are 14 [15: 17: 19: 21] sts on right
needle, turn and leave rem sts on a stitch holder. Work each
side of neck separately.
Next row: Cast off 3 sts, patt to end.
Cast off rem 11 [12: 14: 16: 18] sts.
With RS facing, rejoin yarn to rem sts, cast off centre
31 [31: 33: 33: 35] sts, patt to end.
Complete to match first side reversing shaping.

FRONT

Work as given for back until 16 [16: 18: 18: 20] rows less
have been worked than on back to start of shoulder shaping,
ending with RS facing for next row.
Shape neck
Next row (RS): Patt 28 [31: 35: 40: 44], turn and leave rem
sts on a holder. Work each side of neck separately.
Work 1 row.
Dec 1 st at neck edge in next 5 rows, then on 2 [2: 3: 3: 4]
foll alt rows. 21 [24: 27: 32: 35] sts.
Work 5 rows straight, ending with RS facing for next row.
(Work should now match back to start of shoulder shaping.)
Shape shoulder
Next row (RS): Cast off 10 [12: 13: 16: 17] sts, patt to end.
Work 1 row.
Cast off rem 11 [12: 14: 16: 18] sts.
With RS facing, rejoin yarn to rem sts, cast off centre 23 sts,
patt to end.
Complete to match first side reversing shaping.

SLEEVES (BOTH ALIKE)

Using 6mm (US 10) needles cast on 61 [65: 67: 71: 73] sts.
Knit 2 rows.
Change to 7mm (US 10½) needles and cont as folls:
Row 1 (RS): K0 [2: 3: 5: 0], K2togtbl, ★ K4, (K1, yon, K1)
into next st, K4, sl 1, K2tog, psso, rep from ★ to last 11 [13:
14: 16: 11] sts, K4, (K1, yon, K1) into next st, K4, K2tog, K0

[2: 3: 5: 0].

Row 2: Purl.

These 2 rows form patt.

Cont in patt until sleeve meas 24 [25: 26: 26: 26] cm, ending with RS facing for next row.

Cast off 8 [9: 9: 10: 10] sts at beg of next 6 rows.

13 [11: 13: 11: 13] sts.

Cast off rem sts.

MAKING UP

Press as described on the information page.

Join right shoulder seam using back stitch, or mattress stitch if preferred.

Neckband

With RS facing, using 6mm (US 10) needles, pick up and knit 14 [14: 16: 16: 18] sts down left side of neck, 23 sts from centre front neck, 14 [14: 16: 16: 18] sts up right side of neck and 36 [36: 38: 38: 40] sts across back neck.

87 [87: 93: 93: 99] sts.

Row 1 (WS): P1, ★ K1, P1, rep from ★ to end.

Row 2: ★ K1, P1, rep from ★ to last st, K1.

These 2 rows form rib.

Work 3 rows more in rib.

Cast off in rib.

Join left shoulder and neckband seam. Join side seams and sew in sleeves using the drop shoulder method.

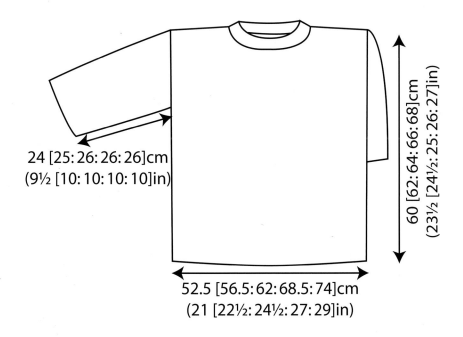

24 [25: 26: 26: 26]cm
(9½ [10: 10: 10: 10]in)

60 [62: 64: 66: 68]cm
(23½ [24½: 25: 26: 27]in)

52.5 [56.5: 62: 68.5: 74]cm
(21 [22½: 24½: 27: 29]in)

SIZE

S	M	L	XL	XXL	
To fit bust					
81–86	91–96	102–107	112–117	122–127	cm
32–34	36–38	40–42	44–46	48–50	in

YARN

Rowan Colourscape

5	6	6	7	7 x	100gm

(photographed in Northern Lights 436)

NEEDLES

1 pair 7mm (no 2) (US 10½) needles, 1 pair 6mm (no 4) (US 10) needles
Stitch holder

BUTTONS

2 x BN1360 by Bedecked

TENSION

14 sts and 18 rows to 10cm measured over st st using 7mm (no 2)
(US 10½) needles.

BACK

Using 6mm (US 10) needles cast on 66 [73: 82: 90: 99] sts.
Knit 18 rows.
Change to 7mm (US 10½) needles.
Beg with a K row and working in st st throughout, cont until
work meas 35 [36: 37: 38: 39]cm, ending with RS facing for
next row.
Shape armholes
Cast off 4 [5: 6: 7: 8] sts at beg of next 2 rows.
58 [63: 70:
76: 83] sts.
Dec 1 st at each end of next 3 [5: 5: 7: 7] rows, then on
2 [1: 2: 1: 2] foll alt rows. 48 [51: 56: 60: 65] sts.
Cont straight until armhole meas 21 [22: 23: 24: 25]cm,
ending with RS facing for next row.
Shape shoulders and back neck
Next row: Cast off 5 [6: 7: 8: 9] sts, K until there are
9 [9: 10: 11: 12] sts on needle, turn and leave rem sts on a
holder.
Work each side of neck separately.
Next row (WS): Cast off 3 sts, P to end. 6 [6: 7: 8: 9] sts.
Cast off rem 6 [6: 7: 8: 9] sts.
With RS facing, rejoin yarn to rem sts, cast off centre
20 [21: 22: 22: 23] sts, K to end.
Complete to match first side reversing all shapings.

LEFT FRONT

Using 6mm (US 10) needles cast on 107 [114: 120:
126: 133] sts.
Place marker on 35th [39th: 43rd: 47th: 52nd] st.
Next row (RS): K to within 1 st of marker, slip next 2 sts
knitways, K1, p2sso, K to end. 105 [112: 118: 124: 131] sts.
Next row: K to marked st, P1, K to end.
Rep these 2 rows 8 times more. 89 [96: 102: 108: 115] sts.
Next row: K26 [30: 34: 38: 43] sts, cast off rem sts.
Change to 7mm (US 10½) needles.
With **WS** facing, rejoin yarn to these 26 [30: 34: 38: 43] sts
and starting with a P row, cont in st st until left front matches
back to start of armhole shaping, ending with RS facing for
next row.
Shape armhole
Next row: Cast off 4 [5: 6: 7: 8] sts, K to end.
22 [25: 28:31: 35] sts.
Work 1 row.
Dec 1 st at armhole edge on next 3 [5: 5: 7: 7] rows, then on
2 [1: 2: 1: 2] foll alt rows. 17 [19: 21: 23: 26] sts.
Cont straight until 18 [18: 20: 20: 22] rows less have been
worked than on back to start of shoulder shaping, ending
with RS facing for next row.
Shape neck
Dec 1 st at neck edge on next row, then 3 [5: 4: 4: 5] foll alt
rows, then on 2 [1: 2: 2: 2] foll 4th rows.

11 [12: 14: 16: 18] sts.

Work 3 rows straight, ending with RS facing for next row.

Shape shoulder

Next row: Cast off 5 [6: 7: 8: 9] sts, K to end.

6 [6: 7: 8: 9] sts.

Work 1 row.

Cast off rem 6 [6: 7: 8: 9] sts.

RIGHT FRONT

Using 6mm (US 10) needles cast on 107 [114: 120: 126: 133] sts.

Place marker on 73rd [76th : 78th : 80th: 82nd] st.

Next row (RS): K to within 1 st of marker, slip next 2 sts knitways, K1, p2sso, K to end. 105 [112: 118: 124: 131] sts.

Next row: K to marked st, P1, K to end.

Rep these 2 rows 8 times more. 89 [96: 102: 108: 115] sts.

Next row: Cast off 63 [66: 68: 70: 72] sts, K to end.

26 [30: 34: 38: 43] sts.

Change to 7mm (US 10½) needles and complete to match left front, reversing all shapings.

SLEEVES

Using 6mm (US 10) needles cast on 28 [28 :31: 31: 33] sts.

Knit 4 rows.

Change to 7mm (US 10½) needles.

Beg with a K row and working in st st throughout, inc 1 st at each end of 5th then 3 [2: 1: 1: 1] foll 6th rows, then on every foll 8th row to 48 [48: 51: 51: 53] sts.

Cont straight until sleeve meas 46 [47: 48: 48: 48]cm, ending with RS facing for next row.

Shape sleeve top

Cast off 4 [5: 6: 7: 8] sts at beg of next 2 rows.

40 [38: 39: 37: 37] sts.

Dec 1 st at each end of next 5 [5: 5: 5: 3] rows, then on 5 [8: 8: 8: 10] foll alt rows, then on 5 [1: 1: 1: 1] foll rows.

10 [10: 11: 9: 9] sts.

Cast off rem 10 [10: 11: 9: 9] sts.

MAKING UP

Press as described on the information page.

Join shoulder seams using back stitch or mattress stitch if preferred. Sew g st border in position up front edge to start of front shaping.

Collar

Using 6mm (US 10) needles, starting 2cm in from front edge pick up and knit 24 [24: 26: 26: 28] sts evenly up right neck, 26 [26: 28: 28: 28] sts from back neck, and 24 [24: 26: 26:28] sts down left neck, ending 2cm in from front edge. 74 [74: 80: 80: 84] sts.

Knit 4 rows.

Change to 7mm (US 10½) needles and cont in g st until collar meas 10cm, ending with RS facing for next row.

Next row: K19 [19: 22: 22: 24], (M1, K4) 9 times, M1, K to end. 84 [84: 90: 90: 94] sts.

Cont in g st until collar meas 14cm, ending with **WS** facing for next row.

Cast off knitways (on **WS**).

Buttonloops

Using 6mm (US 10) needles cast on 13 sts.

Cast off.

Join side and underarm seams. Sew buttonloops and buttons in position as shown.

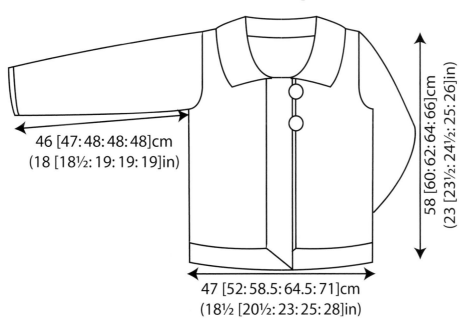

46 [47: 48: 48: 48]cm
(18 [18½: 19: 19: 19]in)

58 [60: 62: 64: 66]cm
(23 [23½: 24½: 25: 26]in)

47 [52: 58.5: 64.5: 71]cm
(18½ [20½: 23: 25: 28]in)

SIZE

	S	M	L	XL	XXL	
To fit bust						
	81–86	91–96	102–107	112–117	122–127	cm
	32–34	36–38	40–42	44–46	48–50	in

YARN

Rowan Colourscape

4	4	5	5	6 x	100gm

(photographed in Spring)

NEEDLES

1 pair 7mm (no 2) (US 10½) needles, 1 pair 6mm (no 4) (US 10) needles
Stitch holder

TENSION

14 sts and 18 rows to 10cm measured over st st using 7mm (no 2) (US 10½) needles.

SPECIAL ABBREVIATIONS

M1P – pick up loop between last and next st and P into the back of this loop

BACK

Using 6mm (US 10) needles cast on 65 [71: 79: 89: 97] sts.
Row 1 (RS): K1, ★ P1, K1, rep from ★ to end.
Row 2: ★ P1, K1, rep from ★ to last st, P1.
These 2 rows form rib.
Work 4 rows more in rib.
Change to 7mm (US 10½) needles.
Beg with a P row and working in rev st st throughout, cont until work meas 25 [26: 27: 28:29]cm, ending with RS facing for next row.
Shape sleeve
Next row (RS): P2, M1P, P to last 2 sts, M1P, P2.
67 [73: 81: 91: 99] sts.
This row sets sleeve shaping.
Inc 1 st as set at each end of 4 foll alt rows.
75 [81: 89: 99: 107] sts.
Place markers at each end of last row to denote start of armhole.
Cont straight until armhole meas 23 [24: 25: 26: 27]cm from markers, ending with RS facing
Shape shoulders and back neck

Next row (RS): Cast off 7 [8: 9: 11: 12] sts, P until there are 21 [23: 25: 28: 30] sts on right needle, turn and leave rem sts on a holder.
Work each side of neck separately.
Next row (WS): Cast off 3 sts, K to end.
18 [20: 22: 25: 27] sts.
Next row: Cast off 7 [8: 9: 11: 12] sts, P to end.
11 [12: 13: 14: 15] sts.
Next row: Cast off 3 sts, K to end. 8 [9: 10: 11: 12] sts.
Cast off rem 8 [9: 10: 11: 12] sts.
With RS facing, rejoin yarn to rem sts, cast off centre 19 [19: 21: 21: 23] sts, P to end.
Complete to match first side, reversing shapings.

LEFT FRONT

Using 6mm (US 10) needles cast on 34 [38: 42: 46: 50] sts.
Row 1 (RS): K1, ★ P1, K1, rep from ★ to last st, K1.
Row 2: ★ K1, P1, rep from ★ to end.
These 2 rows form rib and g st edging.
Work 4 rows more as set.
Change to 7mm (US 10½) needles.
Row 1 (RS): P to last 4 sts, K1, P1, K2.
Row 2: (K1, P1) twice, K to end.
These 2 rows set rev st st and front edging.
Cont as set until work meas 25 [26: 27: 28: 29]cm, ending with RS facing for next row.

Shape sleeve

Next row (RS): P2, M1P, patt to end. 35 [39: 43: 47: 51] sts.
This row sets sleeve shaping.
Inc 1 st as set at beg of 4 foll alt rows. 39 [43: 47: 51: 55] sts.
Place marker at beg of last row to denote start of armhole.
Work 4 rows straight, ending with **WS** facing for next row.

Shape neck

Next row (WS): Cast off 5 [6: 6: 6: 6] sts, K to end.
34 [37: 41: 45: 49] sts.
Dec 1 st at neck edge in next and 8 [7: 9: 7: 7] foll alt rows,
then on every foll 4th row to 22 [25: 28: 33: 36] sts.
Cont straight until armhole matches back to start of shoulder
shaping, ending with RS facing for next row.

Shape shoulder

Cast off 7 [8: 9: 11: 12] sts at beg of next and foll alt row.
8 [9: 10: 11: 12] sts.
Work 1 row.
Cast off rem 8 [9: 10: 11: 12] sts.

RIGHT FRONT

Using 6mm (US 10) needles cast on 34 [38: 42: 46: 50] sts.

Row 1 (RS): K1, ★ K1, P1, rep from ★ to last st, K1.

Row 2: ★ P1, K1, rep from ★ to end.
These 2 rows form g st edging and rib.
Work 4 rows more as set.
Change to 7mm (US 10½) needles.

Row 1 (RS): K2, P1, K1, P to end.

Row 2: K to last 4 sts, (P1, K1) twice.
These 2 rows set front edging and rev st st.
Complete to match left front, reversing all shapings.

MAKING UP

Press as described on the information page.
Join shoulder seams using back stitch or mattress stitch if
preferred.

Neck Tie

Using 6mm (US 10) needles, cast on 11 sts.

Row 1 (RS): K2, ★P1, K1, rep from ★ to last st, K1.

Row 2: ★ K1, P1, rep from ★ to last st, K1.
These 2 rows form rib.
Work 2 rows more in rib.

Row 5 (RS): K2, P1, knit to last 3 sts, P1, K2.

Row 6. K1, P1, K1, purl to last 3 sts, K1, P1, K1.
These 2 rows form patt, cont in patt as set until tie meas
28cm, ending with RS facing for next row.
Place marker at beg of last row.

Next row: Patt 3, K to end.

Next row: P to last 3 sts, patt 3.

Rep last 2 rows until tie, from marker and unstretched, fits up
entire right front slope, across back neck and down left front
slope and ending with RS facing for next row. Place a marker
at beg of last row.
Now rep rows 5 and 6 until tie meas 25cm, ending with RS
facing.
Work 4 rows in rib as given for left front.
Beg and ending at front neck shaping, slip stitch neck tie all
round neck edge between markers.

ARMHOLE BORDERS (Both alike)

Using 6mm (US 10) needles, pick up and knit 73 [77: 81: 85:
89] sts evenly around armhole edge.
Starting with 2nd row of rib as given for back, work 5 rows in
rib.
Cast off in rib.

Join side and underarm seams.

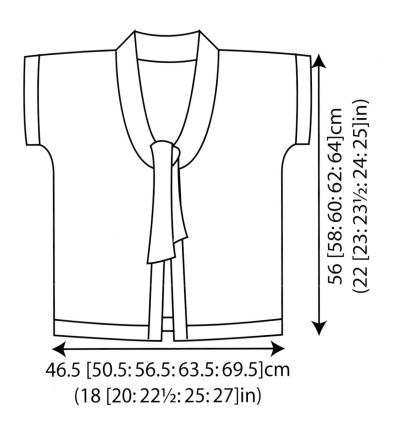

46.5 [50.5: 56.5: 63.5: 69.5]cm
(18 [20: 22½: 25: 27]in)

56 [58: 60: 62: 64]cm
(22 [23: 23½: 24: 25]in)

Polly

SIZE

S	M	L	XL	XXL	
To fit bust					
81-86	91-96	102-107	112-117	122-127	cm
32-34	36-38	40-42	44-46	48-50	in

YARN

Rowan Colourscape

4	4	5	5	6 x	100gm

(photographed in Ghost 435)

NEEDLES

1 pair 7mm (no 2) (US 10½) needles, 1 pair 6mm (no 4) (US 10) needles
1 6mm (no 4) (US 10) circular needle
Stitch holder

TENSION

14 sts and 18 rows to 10cm measured over st st using 7mm (no 2) (US 10½) needles.

FRONT

Using 6mm (US 10) needles cast on 66 [70: 78: 86: 98] sts.

Row 1 (RS): K2, ★ P2, K2, rep from ★ to end.

Row 2: ★ P2, K2, rep from ★ to last 2 sts, P2.

These 2 rows form rib.

Work 22 rows more in rib, dec 1 [0: 0: 0: 1] st at each end of last row. 64 [70: 78: 86: 96] sts.

Change to 7mm (US 10½) needles. ★★

Beg with a K row and working in st st throughout, cont as folls:-

Next row (RS): K28 [31: 35: 39: 44], turn and leave rem sts on a holder.

Work each side of neck separately.

Next row: Cast on 8 sts, P to end. 36 [39: 43: 47: 52] sts.

Next row: K to last 4 sts, K2tog, K2.

This row sets front edge shaping.

Dec 1 st at neck edge as set on 2nd and 4 [4: 3: 4: 3] foll alt rows, then on 7 [7: 8: 8: 9] foll 4th rows. 23 [26: 30: 33: 38] sts.

Work 1 [3: 3: 3: 3] rows without shaping, ending with RS facing for next row.

Shape armhole

Next row: Cast off 4 [5: 6: 6: 7] sts, K to last 0 [4: 4: 4: 4] sts, K2tog 0 [1: 1: 1: 1] time, K0 [2: 2: 2: 2] sts.

19 [20: 23: 26: 30] sts.

Work 1 row.

Dec 1 st at armhole edge on next 3 [3: 3: 5: 7] rows, then on 1 [1: 2: 2: 2] foll alt rows **and at same time** dec 1 st at neck edge as set on 1st [3rd: 3rd: 3rd : 3rd] and 1 [-: 1: 1: 2] foll 4th [-: 4th: 4th :4th] rows . 13 [15: 16: 17: 18] sts.

Dec 1 st at neck edge only on 4th [2nd:4th:2nd :4th] and every foll 4th row to 9 [11: 12: 14: 15] sts.

Cont straight until armhole meas 21 [22: 23: 24: 25]cm, ending with RS facing for next row.

Shape shoulder

Next row: Cast off 4 [5: 6: 7: 7] sts, K to end.

Work 1 row.

Cast off rem 5 [6: 6: 7: 8] sts.

With RS facing, rejoin yarn to rem 36 [39: 43: 47: 52] sts, K to end.

Work 1 row.

Next row: K2, sl 1, K1, psso, K to end.

This row sets front edge shaping.

Complete to match first side reversing shapings.

BACK

Work as given for Front to ★★.

Beg with a K row and working in st st throughout, cont until work matches front to start of armhole shaping, ending with RS facing for next row.

Shape armhole

Cast off 4 [5: 6: 6: 7] sts at beg of next 2 rows.

56 [60: 66: 74: 82] sts.

Dec 1 st at each end of next 3 [3: 3: 5: 7] rows, then on 1 [1: 2: 2: 2] foll alt rows. 48 [52: 56: 60: 64] sts.

Cont straight until armhole matches front to start of shoulder shaping, ending with RS facing for next row. ~30 rows

Shape shoulders and back neck

Next row: Cast off 4 [5: 6: 7: 7] sts, K until there are 8 [9: 9: 10: 11] sts on needle, turn and leave rem sts on a holder. Work each side of neck separately.

Next row (WS): Cast off 3 sts, P to end. 5 [6: 6: 7: 8] sts. Cast off rem 5 [6: 6: 7: 8] sts.

With RS facing, rejoin yarn to rem sts, cast off centre 24 [24: 26: 26: 28] sts, K to end.

Complete to match first side of neck reversing shapings.

SLEEVES

Using 6mm (US 10) needles cast on 30 [30: 30: 30: 34] sts. Work 12 rows in rib as given for back, dec 1 [1: 0: 0: 1] st at each end of last row. 28 [28: 30: 30: 32] sts.

Change to 7mm (US 10½) needles.

Beg with a K row and working in st st throughout, inc 1 st at each end of 5th row, then 7 [7: 6: 6: 10] foll 6th rows, then on every foll 8th [8th: 8th: 8th: –] row to 48 [48: 50: 50: 54] sts. 44 sts.

Cont straight until sleeve meas 46 [47: 48: 48: 48]cm, ending with RS facing for next row. 11 rows

Shape sleeve top

Cast off 4 [5: 6: 7: 7] sts at beg of next 2 rows.

40 [38: 38: 36: 40] sts.

Dec 1 st at each end of next 5 [5: 5: 5: 3] rows, then on 5 [8: 8: 8: 10] foll alt rows, then on 5 [1: 1: 1: 1] foll rows. 10 [10: 10: 8: 12] sts.

Cast off rem 10 [10: 10: 8: 12] sts.

MAKING UP

Press as described on the information page.

Join shoulder seams using back stitch, or mattress stitch if preferred.

Neckband

Using 6mm (USA 10) circular needle, pick up and knit 69 [73: 76: 80: 85] sts evenly up right front edge, 30 [30: 32: 32: 34] sts from back neck, and 69 [73: 76: 80: 85] sts down left front edge. 168 [176: 184: 192: 204] sts.

Row 1 (WS): K1, ★ P2, K2, rep from ★ to last 3 sts, P2, K1.

Row 2: P1, K2, ★ P2, K2, rep from ★ to last st, P1.

These 2 rows form rib.

Cont 10 rows more in rib.

Cast off in rib.

Placing right front over left front sew front borders in position.

Join side and underarm seams.

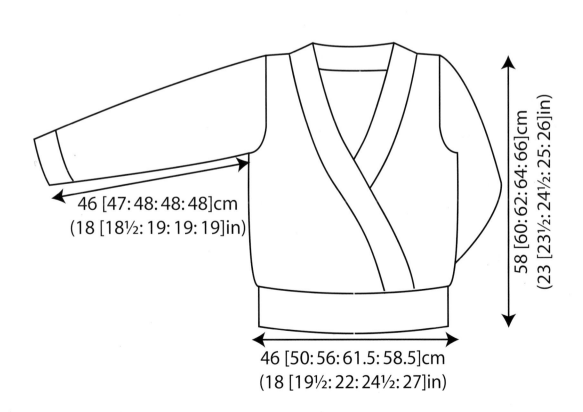

46 [47: 48: 48: 48]cm
(18 [18½: 19: 19: 19]in)

58 [60: 62: 64: 66]cm
(23 [23½: 24½: 25: 26]in)

46 [50: 56: 61.5: 58.5]cm
(18 [19½: 22: 24½: 27]in)

Lilly

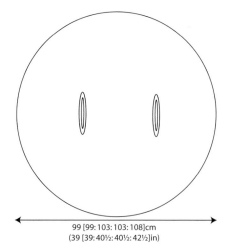

SIZE

S	M	L	XL	XXL	
To fit bust					
81-86	91-96	102-107	112-117	122-127	cm
32-34	36-38	40-42	44-46	48-50	in

YARN

Rowan Colourscape

3	4	4	5	5 x	100gm

(photographed in Cherry)

NEEDLES

1 pair 7mm (no 2) (US 10½) needles, 1 6mm (no 4) (US 10) circular needle

BUTTONS

1 Small Kilt Pin

TENSION

14 sts and 18 rows to 10cm measured over st st using 7mm (no 2) (US 10½) needles.

SPECIAL ABBREVIATIONS

M1 – pick up loop between last and next st and K into the back of this loop

Using 7mm (US 10) needles cast on 8 sts.
Row 1 (RS): ⋆ K1, M1, rep from ⋆ to last st, K1. 15 sts.
Row 2: Purl.
Row 3: ⋆ K2, M1, rep from ⋆ to last st, K1. 22 sts.
Row 4: Purl.
Row 5: ⋆ K3, M1, rep from ⋆ to last st, K1. 29 sts.
Row 6: Purl.
These 6 rows set increasing.
Work 38 [38: 40: 40: 42] rows more as set, working an extra st in each 'section' each time. 162 [162: 169: 169: 176] sts.
Shape armholes
Next row: K23 [23: 24: 24: 25], M1, K10 [9: 9: 8: 8], cast off 26 [28: 30: 32: 34] sts, K until there are 10 [9: 9: 8: 8] sts on right needle after cast off, M1, K23 [23: 24: 24: 25], M1, K10 [9: 9: 8: 8], cast off 26 [28: 30: 32: 34] sts, K until there are 10 [9: 9: 8: 8] sts on right needle after cast off, M1, K23 [23: 24: 24: 25], M1, K1.
Next row: P to gap left by first set of cast off sts, cast on 27 [29: 31: 33: 35], P to next set of cast off sts, cast on 27 [29: 31: 33: 35], P to end. 169 [169: 176: 176: 183] sts.
Working increases as set, work a further 40 [40: 42: 42: 44] rows, ending with RS facing for next row.
309 [309: 323: 323: 337] sts.
Cont as folls:-
Next row (RS): K1, ⋆ P1, K1, rep from ⋆ to end.

Next row: ⋆ P1, K1, rep from ⋆ to last st, P1.
These 2 rows set 1 x 1 rib, work 1 row more in rib.
Cast off in rib loosely on **WS**.

ARMHOLE EDGES

With RS facing, using 6mm (US 10) circular needle pick up and knit 61 [63: 65: 67: 69] sts around cast off and cast off edges of armhole.
Starting with 2nd row of rib as set on body, work 3 rows.
Cast off in rib.

MAKING UP

PRESS as described on the information page.
Join seam to form a circle, using back stitch or mattress stitch if preferred, (this seam will fall at the lower centre back in wear).

99 [99: 103: 103: 108]cm
(39 [39: 40½: 40½: 42½]in)

sizing guide

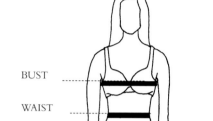

BUST

WAIST

HIPS

Our sizing now conforms to standard clothing sizes. Therefore if you buy a standard size 12 in clothing, then our size 12 or Medium patterns will fit you perfectly.

Dimensions in the charts shown are body measurements, not garment dimensions, therefore please refer to the measuring guide to help you to determine which is the best size for you to knit.

CASUAL SIZING GUIDE FOR WOMEN

As there are some designs that are intended to fit more generously, we have introduced our casual sizing guide. The designs that fall into this group can be recognised by the size range: Small, Medium, Large, Xlarge & XXlarge. Each of these sizes cover two sizes from the standard sizing guide, ie. Size S will fit sizes 8/10, size M will fit sizes 12/14 and so on.

The sizing within this chart is also based on the larger size within the range, ie. M will be based on size 14.

UK SIZE DUAL SIZE	S 8/10	M 12/14	L 16/18	XL 20/22	XXL 24/26	
To fit bust	32 – 34	36 – 38	40 – 42	44 – 46	48-50	inches
	81 – 86	91 – 97	102 – 107	112 – 117	122/127	cm
To fit waist	24 – 26	28 – 30	32 – 34	36 – 38	40-42	inches
	61 – 66	71 – 76	81 – 86	91 – 97	102-107	cm
To fit hips	34 – 36	38 – 40	42 – 44	46 – 48	50-52	inches
	86 – 91	97 – 102	107 – 112	117 – 122	127-132	cm

STANDARD SIZING GUIDE FOR MEN

UK SIZE EUR Size	S 50	M 52	L 54	XL 56	XXL 58	2XL 60	
To fit chest	40	42	44	46	48	50	inches
	102	107	112	117	122	127	cm
To fit waist	32	34	36	38	40	42	inches
	81	86	91	97	102	107	cm

MEASURING GUIDE

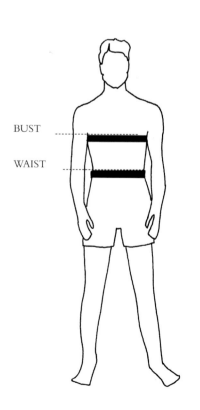

BUST

WAIST

For maximum comfort and to ensure the correct fit when choosing a size to knit, please follow the tips below when checking your size.

Measure yourself close to your body, over your underwear and don't pull the tape measure too tight!

Bust/chest – measure around the fullest part of the bust/chest and across the shoulder blades.

Waist – measure around the natural waistline, just above the hip bone.

Hips – measure around the fullest part of the bottom.

If you don't wish to measure yourself, note the size of a favourite jumper that you like the fit of. Our sizes are now comparable to the clothing sizes from the major high street retailers, so if your favourite jumper is a size Medium or size 12, then our casual size Medium and standard size 12

should be approximately the same fit.

To be extra sure, measure your favourite jumper and then compare these measurements with the Rowan size diagram given at the end of the individual instructions.

Finally, once you have decided which size is best for you, please ensure that you achieve the tension required for the design you wish to knit.

Remember if your tension is too loose, your garment will be bigger than the pattern size and you may use more yarn. If your tension is too tight, your garment could be smaller than the pattern size and you will have yarn left over.

Furthermore if your tension is incorrect, the handle of your fabric will be too stiff or floppy and will not fit properly. It really does make sense to check your tension before starting every project.

information

TENSION

Obtaining the correct tension is perhaps the single factor which can make the difference between a successful garment and a disastrous one. It controls both the shape and size of an article, so any variation, however slight, can distort the finished garment. Different designers feature in our books and it is **their** tension, given at the **start** of each pattern, which you must match. We recommend that you knit a square in pattern and/or stocking stitch (depending on the pattern instructions) of perhaps 5 - 10 more stitches and 5 - 10 more rows than those given in the tension note. Mark out the central 10cm square with pins. If you have too many stitches to 10cm try again using thicker needles, if you have too few stitches to 10cm try again using finer needles. Once you have achieved the correct tension your garment will be knitted to the measurements indicated in the size diagram shown at the end of the pattern.

SIZING & SIZE DIAGRAM NOTE

The instructions are given for the smallest size. Where they vary, work the figures in brackets for the larger sizes. **One set of figures refers to all sizes.** Included with most patterns in this magazine is a **'size diagram'**, of the finished garment and its dimensions. The measurement shown at the bottom of each **'size diagram'** shows the garment width 2.5cm below the armhole shaping. To help you choose the size of garment to knit please refer to the NEW sizing guide.

WORKING A LACE PATTERN

When working a lace pattern it is important to remember that if you are unable to work both the increase and corresponding decrease and vica versa, the stitches should be worked in stocking stitch.

FINISHING INSTRUCTIONS

After working for hours knitting a garment, it seems a great pity that many garments are spoiled because such little care is taken in the pressing and finishing process. Follow the following tips for a truly professional-looking garment.

PRESSING

Block out each piece of knitting and following the instructions on the ball band press the garment pieces, omitting the ribs. Tip: Take special care to press the edges, as this will make sewing up both easier and neater. If the ball band indicates that the fabric is not to be pressed, then covering the blocked out fabric with a damp white cotton cloth and leaving it to stand will have the desired effect. Darn in all ends neatly along the selvage edge or a colour join, as appropriate.

STITCHING

When stitching the pieces together, remember to match areas of texture very carefully where they meet. Use a seam stitch such as back stitch or mattress stitch for all main knitting seams and join all ribs and neckband with mattress stitch, unless otherwise stated. Due to the soft handle of this yarn we would suggest you sew up your garments using a plain yarn in a closely matching colour.

CONSTRUCTION

Having completed the pattern instructions, join left shoulder and neckband seams as detailed above. Sew the top of the sleeve to the body of the garment using the method detailed in the pattern, referring to the appropriate guide:

Straight cast-off sleeves: Place centre of cast-off edge of sleeve to shoulder seam. Sew top of sleeve to body, using markers as guidelines where applicable.

Square set-in sleeves: Place centre of cast-off edge of sleeve to shoulder seam. Set sleeve head into armhole, the straight sides at top of sleeve to form a neat right-angle to cast-off sts at armhole on back and front.

Shallow set-in sleeves: Place centre of cast off edge of sleeve to shoulder seam. Match decreases at beg of armhole shaping to decreases at top of sleeve. Sew sleeve head into armhole, easing in shapings.

Set- in sleeves: Place centre of cast-off edge of sleeve to shoulder seam. Set in sleeve, easing sleeve head into armhole.

Join side and sleeve seams.
Slip stitch pocket edgings and linings into place. Sew on buttons to correspond with buttonholes. Ribbed welts and neckbands and any areas of garter stitch should not be pressed.

Easy, straight forward knitting

Suitable for the average knitter

Suitable for the experienced knitter

ABBREVIATIONS

K	knit
P	purl
st(s)	stitch(es)
inc	increas(e)(ing)
dec	decreas(e)(ing)
st st	stocking stitch (1 row K , 1 row P)
g st	garter stitch (K every row)
beg	begin(ning)
foll	following
rem	remain(ing)
rev st st	reverse stocking stitch (1 row K , 1 row P)
rep	repeat
alt	alternate
cont	continue
patt	pattern
tog	together
mm	millimetres
cm	centimetres
in(s)	inch(es)
RS	right side
WS	wrong side
sl 1	slip one stitch
psso	pass slipped stitch over
p2sso	pass 2 slipped stitches over
tbl	through back of loop
M1	make one stitch by picking up horizontal loop before next stitch and knitting into back of it
M1P	make one stitch by picking up horizontal loop before next stitch and purling into back of it
yfwd	yarn forward
yrn	yarn round needle
meas	measures
0	no stitches, times or rows
-	no stitches, times or rows for that size
yon	yarn over needle
yfrn	yarn forward round needle
wyib	with yarn at back

stockists

AUSTRALIA: Australian Country Spinners, Pty Ltd, Level 7, 409 St. Kilda Road, Melbourne Vic 3004.
Tel: 03 9380 3830 Fax: 03 9820 0989 Email: sales@auspinners.com.au

AUSTRIA: Coats Harlander GmbH, Autokaderstrasse 31, A -1210 Wien. Tel: (01) 27716 – 0 Fax: (01) 27716 - 228

BELGIUM: Coats Benelux, Ring Oost 14A, Ninove, 9400, Belgium
Tel: 0346 35 37 00 Email: sales.coatsninove@coats.com

CANADA: Westminster Fibers Inc, 165 Ledge St, Nashua, NH03060
Tel: (1 603) 886 5041 / 5043 Fax: (1 603) 886 1056
Email: rowan@westminsterfibers.com

CHINA: Coats Shanghai Ltd, No 9 Building , Baosheng Road, Songjiang Industrial Zone, Shanghai. Tel: (86- 21) 5774 3733 Fax: (86-21) 5774 3768

DENMARK: Coats Danmark A/S, Nannasgade 28, 2200 Kobenhavn N
Tel: (45) 35 86 90 50 Fax: (45) 35 82 15 10
Email: info@hpgruppen.dk Web: www.hpgruppen.dk

FINLAND: Coats Opti Oy, Ketjutie 3, 04220 Kerava
Tel: (358) 9 274 871 Fax: (358) 9 2748 7330
Email: coatsopti.sales@coats.com

FRANCE: Coats France / Steiner Frères, SAS 100, avenue du Général de Gaulle, 18 500 Mehun-Sur-Yèvre
Tel: (33) 02 48 23 12 30 Fax: (33) 02 48 23 12 40

GERMANY: Coats GmbH, Kaiserstrasse 1, D-79341 Kenzingen
Tel: (49) 7644 8020 Fax: (49) 7644 802399 Web: www.coatsgmbh.de

HOLLAND: Coats Benelux, Ring Oost 14A, Ninove, 9400, Belgium
Tel: 0346 35 37 00 Email: sales.coatsninove@coats.com

HONG KONG: Coats China Holdings Ltd, 19/F Millennium City 2, 378 Kwun Tong Road, Kwun Tong, Kowloon
Tel: (852) 2798 6886 Fax: (852) 2305 0311

ICELAND: Storkurinn, Laugavegi 59, 101 Reykjavik
Tel: (354) 551 8258 Email: storkurinn@simnet.is

ITALY: Coats Cucirini s.r.l.,Via Sarca 223, 20126 Milano
Tel: 800 992377 Fax: 0266111701 Email: servizio.clienti@coats.com

KOREA: Coats Korea Co Ltd, 5F Kuckdong B/D, 935-40
Bangbae - Dong, Seocho-Gu, Seoul
Tel: (82) 2 521 6262 Fax: (82) 2 521 5181

LEBANON: y.knot, Saifi Village, Mkhalissiya Street 162, Beirut
Tel: (961) 1 992211 Fax: (961) 1 315553 Email: y.knot@cyberia.net.lb

LUXEMBOURG: Coats Benelux, Ring Oost 14A, Ninove, 9400, Belgium Tel: 054 318989 Email: sales.coatsninove@coats.com

MEXICO: Estambres Crochet SA de CV, Aaron Saenz 1891-7, Monterrey, NL 64650 Mexico Tel: +52 (81) 8335-3870

NEW ZEALAND: ACS New Zealand, 1 March Place, Belfast, Christchurch Tel: 64-3-323-6665 Fax: 64-3-323-6660

NORWAY: Coats Knappehuset AS, Pb 100 Ulset, 5873 Bergen
Tel: (47) 55 53 93 00 Fax: (47) 55 53 93 93

SINGAPORE: Golden Dragon Store, 101 Upper Cross Street #02-51, People's Park Centre, Singapore 058357
Tel: (65) 6 5358454 Fax: (65) 6 2216278 Email: gdscraft@hotmail.com

SOUTH AFRICA: Arthur Bales PTY, PO Box 44644, Linden 2104
Tel: (27) 11 888 2401 Fax: (27) 11 782 6137

SPAIN: Oyambre, Pau Claris 145, 80009 Barcelona.
Tel: (34) 670 011957 Fax: (34) 93 4872672
Email: oyambre@oyambreonline.com

Coats Fabra, Santa Adria 20, 08030 Barcelona
Tel: 932908400 Fax: 932908409 Email: atencion.clientes@coats.com

SWEDEN: Coats Expotex AB, Division Craft, Box 297, 401 24 Goteborg
Tel: (46) 33 720 79 00 Fax: 46 31 47 16 50

SWITZERLAND: Coats Stroppel AG, Stroppelstr.16
CH -5300 Turgi (AG) Tel: (41) 562981220 Fax: (41) 56 298 12 50

TAIWAN: Cactus Quality Co Ltd, P.O.Box 30 485, Taipei, Taiwan, R.O.C., Office: 7FL-2, No 140, Roosevelt Road, Sec 2, Taipei, Taiwan, R.O.C.
Tel: 886-2-23656527 Fax: 886-2-23656503 Email: cqcl@m17.hinet.net

THAILAND: Global Wide Trading, 10 Lad Prao Soi 88, Bangkok 10310
Tel: 00 662 933 9019 Fax: 00 662 933 9110
Email: theneedleworld@yahoo.com

U.S.A.: Westminster Fibers Inc, 165 Ledge St, Nashua, NH03060
Tel: (1 603) 886 5041 / 5043 Fax: (1 603) 886 1056
Email: rowan@westminsterfibers.com

U.K: Rowan, Green Lane Mill, Holmfirth, West Yorkshire, England HD9 2DX
Tel: +44 (0) 1484 681881 Fax: +44 (0) 1484 687920
Email: mail@knitrowan.com Web: www.knitrowan.com

For stockists in all other countries please contact Rowan for details

ROWAN

Photographer	•	Daniel Halpin
Art Direction & Sylist	•	Rowan
Hair & Make-up	•	Jeni Dodson
Models	•	Martha at M&P Models, Konrad at FM Models & Leonado at Storm
Design Layout	•	Rowan
Location	•	MC Motors
Handknitters	•	Cindy Noble, Violet Ellis, Jools Yeo, Ella Taylor, Elizabeth Jones, Anne Newton, Ann Holdsworth, Maissie Laing, Margeret Goddard, Barbara Hooper, Val Deaks, Susan Grimes, Jean Flether, Aran Ronan & Lorraine Hearn
Buttons	•	Bedecked Ltd, 1 Castle Wall, Back Fold, Hay-On-Wye, Via Hereford, HR3 5EQ

shop tel: 01497 822769
web: www.bedecked.co.uk
email: thegirls@bedecked.co.uk

Bedecked
fine trimmings

First published in Great Britain in 2009 by Rowan Yarns Ltd, Green Lane Mill, Holmfirth, West Yorkshire, England, HD9 2DX
Internet: www.knitrowan.com
© Copyright Rowan 2009
British Library Cataloguing in Publication Data Rowan Yarns – Colourscape Folk
ISBN 978-1-906007-68-3